*On the
Advantage
and
Disadvantage
of History
for Life*

FRIEDRICH NIETZSCHE

On the Advantage and Disadvantage of History for Life

Translated, with an Introduction,
by PETER PREUSS

HACKETT PUBLISHING COMPANY, INC.
Indianapolis • Cambridge

Friedrich Nietzsche: 1844–1900
Vom Nutzen und Nachteil der Historie für das Leben
was first published in 1874.

For further information, please address

HACKETT PUBLISHING COMPANY, INC.
Box 44937
Indianapolis, Indiana 46244-0937

Library of Congress Cataloging in Publication Data

Nietzsche, Friedrich Wilhelm, 1844–1900.
   On the advantage and disadvantage of history for
life.

   Translation of the author's Vom Nutzen und Nachteil
der Historie für das Leben, which is part 2 of his
Unzeitgemässe Betrachtungen.
   1.   Strauss, David Friedrich, 1808–1874.
2.   History—Study and teaching.   3.   Schopenhauer,
Arthur, 1788–1860.   4.   Wagner, Richard, 1813–1883.
I.   Title.
B3313.U52E5   1980   128   80-16686
ISBN 0-915144-95-6
ISBN 0-915144-94-8 (pbk.)

The paper used in this publication meets the minimum requirements of
American National Standard for Information Sciences—Permanence of
Paper for Printed Library Materials, ANSI Z39.48-1984.

CONTENTS

INTRODUCTION

Man, unlike the animal, is self-conscious. He is aware that he is alive and that he must die. And because he is self-conscious he is not only aware of living, but of living well or badly. Life is not wholly something that happens to man; it is also something he engages in according to values he follows. Human existence is a task. In the past two centuries or so of European philosophizing there have been a number of attempts to clarify this task: the Hegelian elevation of individual finitude into infinity in the Absolute; the Kierkegaardian life of inwardness; and the Heideggerian authentic life of preparation for the self-revelation of Being, among others.

Nietzsche, too, understands human existence to be a task. He calls it simply the task of living. As with any genuine philosophy of this kind, his attempt to clarify philosophically the task of human existence is itself always a part of that task. It is not written from an assumed standpoint outside of human existence, merely viewing that existence dispassionately and objectively, but is written from the standpoint of a human being engaged in this task, fully aware that he is so engaged.

Not only is Nietzsche aware that philosophizing is part of the task of existence; he also insists that every human enterprise is a part of the task. Whatever a person does finally receives its meaning only so far as it is integrated into the total task of existing. If it fails to further this task it is valueless. If it hinders this task it is to be rejected.

The topic of the present work is the relation between life and historical knowledge. The quest for knowledge and truth is also a part of the task of existing and, like every human enterprise, it receives its value from being integrated into the task of which it is a part. But what if some knowledge, some truth, should prove deadly? What if, with respect to some knowledge, we are faced with the alternative: know the truth and die or live and remain in error? According to Nietzsche we are faced with this alternative. But given the choice between life and knowledge, he argues, there is no question about which we ought to choose. Any knowledge which destroys life destroys itself, for knowledge presupposes life.

The nineteenth century had discovered history and all subsequent inquiry and education bore the stamp of this discovery. This was not simply the discovery of a set of facts about the past but the discovery of the historicity of man: man, unlike the animal, is a historical being. Man is not wholly the product of an alien act, either natural or divine, but in part produces his own being. The task of existing is a task precisely because it is not a case of acting according to a permanent nature or essence but rather of producing that nature within the limitations of a situation. History is the record of this self-production; it is the activity of a historical being recovering the past into a present which anticipates the future. With a

1

total absence of this activity man would fall short of humanity: history is necessary.

But what if this activity is perverted? What if, rather than remaining the life-promoting activity of a historical being, history is turned into the objective uncovering of mere facts by the disinterested scholar — facts to be left as they are found, to be contemplated without being assimilated into present being? According to Nietzsche, this perversion has taken place — and history, rather than promoting life, has become deadly. This, then, is the dilemma Nietzsche faced: history is necessary, but as it is practiced it is deadly. The present work is an attempt to extricate himself, and us, from this dilemma.

For Nietzsche, as for almost every post-Kantian European philosopher, philosophizing is part of the task of existing. That it is such a part shows up in different ways: as dialectical philosophizing in Hegel; as irony and multiple pseudonyms in Kierkegaard; as revolutionary pamphleteering in Marx; as prophetic paths of thinking in Heidegger. In Nietzsche it shows up in the experimental character of his philosophizing. His chief concern with a philosophical position is not so much its intellectual cogency as its ability to stand the test of living by it. This is why, by quoting Nietzsche selectively, one can make a case for the most divergent sorts of positions. For example, the present work is a fine example of Nietzsche's early period (*The Birth of Tragedy*, the four *Untimely Observations* of which the present work is the second). Here he condemns objective scholarship as detrimental to human life which must flourish, if need be, in an atmosphere of error and illusion. But his middle period (*Human, All Too Human; Dawn of Day; The Gay Science*) commences with a radical shift in favour of objective science and the exposing of all illusion. It ends, however, with the tragic realization that God has been killed in the process (*The Gay Science* #125). Having experimented with these two antithetical positions, he understands that neither is tenable. Only a product of their reconciliation can be tenable, and he attempts to achieve this in his late period (*Thus Spoke Zarathustra; Beyond Good and Evil; The Genealogy of Morals; The Antichrist; Twilight of the Idols*). It is because the reconciliation of the late period appears to favour the position of the early period that Nietzsche's middle period has been unduly neglected in favour of the other two. This is unfortunate. But just as unfortunate is the recent about-face in Germany of elevating his middle period to the status of the authentic Nietzschean philosophy and downgrading the rest as either the product of youthful exuberance or tottering reason. Only the total Nietzsche is the total Nietzsche.

On the Advantage and Disadvantage of History for Life is an excellent point of entry into the philosophy of Nietzsche. Not only does it sound many of the main points of the whole, but is a clear statement of the profoundest concerns which animate the whole. If it is understood for what it is it can, better than any other work, provide the foundation for an appropriating study of this powerful thinker.

The University of Lethbridge   PETER PREUSS

TRANSLATOR'S NOTE

I have tried to remain faithful to the text not only by accurately reproducing Nietzsche's meaning but also by preserving his stylistic artistry as much as I was able and English would allow without protest. I have also tried to give footnotes to all quotations and where otherwise helpful. In some cases I failed. With some of my failures there is little loss I think, just as with some of the successes there was little gain. A few of them, however, are regrettable, such as the long quotation from Niebuhr in Section 1, and the equally long one from Grillparzer in Section 6.

Many people have helped me in a number of ways and I here wish to thank the late Professor Dieter Müller of the University of Lethbridge; Professors Ron Gray of Emmanuel College in Cambridge University; M. Gudrun Hesse of the University of Lethbridge; William Hodern of the Lutheran Theological Seminary in the University of Saskatchewan; Wolfgang Leppmann of the University of Oregon; Gerwin Marahrens of the University of Alberta, and librarians Inge Baum of the Library of the Supreme Council 33° in Washington, D.C., Robert R. McCollough of the University of Oregon, and Janet F. White of the University of Michigan.

This book has been published with the help of a grant from the Canadian Federation for the Humanities, using funds provided by the Social Sciences and Humanities Research Council of Canada. I wish to express my gratitude to the Canadian Federation for the Humanities and its able and helpful referees, Professors Harry Zohn of Brandeis University and Peter Heller of State University of New York at Buffalo.

*On the
Advantage
and
Disadvantage
of History
for Life*

ON THE ADVANTAGE AND DISADVANTAGE
OF HISTORY FOR LIFE

Preface

"Moreover I hate everything which merely instructs me without increasing or directly quickening my activity." These are Goethe's words with which, as with a boldly expressed *ceterum censeo*,[1] we may begin our consideration of the worth and worthlessness of history. Our aim will be to show why instruction which fails to quicken activity, why knowledge which enfeebles activity, why history as a costly intellectual excess and luxury must, in the spirit of Goethe's words, be seriously hated; for we still lack what is most necessary, and superfluous excess is the enemy of the necessary. Certainly we need history. But our need for history is quite different from that of the spoiled idler in the garden of knowledge, even if he in his refinement looks down on our rude and graceless requirements and needs. That is, we require history for life and action, not for the smug avoiding of life and action, or even to whitewash a selfish life and cowardly, bad acts. Only so far as history serves life will we serve it: but there is a degree of doing history and an estimation of it which brings with it a withering and degenerating of life: a phenomenon which is now as necessary as it may be painful to bring to consciousness through some remarkable symptoms of our age.

I have made an effort to describe a feeling which has tortured me often enough; I revenge myself on it by making it public. Perhaps this description will give someone occasion to explain to me that he too knows this feeling but that I have not felt it purely and originally enough and have quite failed to articulate it with the confidence and mature experience due it. A few may think so perhaps; but most will tell me that this is a quite perverted, unnatural, repulsive and downright impermissible feeling, even that with this feeling I have shown myself to be quite unworthy of the mighty historical orientation of the age which, as is well known, has been evident for two generations particularly among the Germans. At any rate, my daring to come forward with a natural description of my feeling will sooner promote than injure general propriety, for in doing so I give opportunity to many to pay compliments to this orientation of the age. For my

---

1. This is an allusion to Cato's "Ceterum censeo Carthaginem esse delendam" ("Moreover I am of the opinion that Carthage be destroyed") with which he used to conclude every speech on any topic whatever until he finally goaded the Romans into the third Punic War. Goethe's words are from a letter from him to Friedrich Schiller dated 19 December 1798.

part, however, I gain something I value more highly than general propriety—public instruction and correction about our age.

These reflections are also untimely, because I attempt to understand as a defect, infirmity and shortcoming of the age something of which our age is justifiably proud, its historical education. I even believe that all of us suffer from a consuming historical fever and should at least realize that we suffer from it. If Goethe has said with good reason that with our virtues we also cultivate our faults, and if, as everyone knows, a hypertrophic virtue—which the historical sense of our age seems to me to be—may bring about the decay of a people as much as a hypertrophic vice, one may as well allow me my say. I should not hide the exonerating circumstance that I have for the most part taken the experiences which those painful feelings occasioned in me from myself and have considered those of others only for the sake of comparison; and that further, only so far as I am the nursling of more ancient times, especially the Greek, could I come to have such untimely experiences about myself as a child of the present age. That much I must be allowed to grant myself on the grounds of my profession as a classical philologist. For I do not know what meaning classical philology would have for our age if not to have an untimely effect within it, that is, to act against the age and so have an effect on the age to the advantage, it is to be hoped, of a coming age.

1

Consider the herd grazing before you. These animals do not know what yesterday and today are but leap about, eat, rest, digest and leap again; and so from morning to night and from day to day, only briefly concerned with their pleasure and displeasure, enthralled by the moment and for that reason neither melancholy nor bored. It is hard for a man to see this, for he is proud of being human and not an animal and yet regards its happiness with envy because he wants nothing other than to live like the animal, neither bored nor in pain, yet wants it in vain because he does not want it like the animal. Man may well ask the animal: why do you not speak to me of your happiness but only look at me? The animal does want to answer and say: because I always immediately forget what I wanted to say—but then it already forgot this answer and remained silent: so that man could only wonder.

But he also wondered about himself, that he cannot learn to forget but always remains attached to the past: however far and fast he runs, the chain runs with him. It is astonishing: the moment, here in a wink, gone in a wink, nothing before and nothing after, returns nevertheless as a spectre to disturb the calm of a later moment. Again and again a page loosens in the scroll of time, drops out, and flutters away—and suddenly flutters back again into man's lap. Then man says "I remember" and envies the animal which immediately forgets and sees each moment really die, sink back into deep night extinguished for ever. In this way the animal lives *unhistorically*: for it goes into the present like a number without leaving a curious fraction; it does not know how to dissimulate, hides nothing, appears at every moment fully as what it is and so cannot but be honest. Man on the other hand resists the great and ever greater weight of the past: this oppresses him and bends him sideways, it encumbers his gait like an invisible and sinister burden which, for the sake of appearances, he may deny at times and which in intercourse with his equals he is all too pleased to deny: to excite their envy. This is why he is moved, as though he remembered a lost paradise, when he sees a grazing herd, or, in more intimate proximity, sees a child, which as yet has nothing past to deny, playing between the fences of past and future in blissful blindness. And yet the child's play must be disturbed: only too soon will it be called out of its forgetfulness. Then it comes to understand the phrase "it was", that password with which struggle, suffering and boredom approach man to remind him what his existence basically is—a never to be completed imperfect tense. And when death finally brings longed-for forgetfulness it also robs him of the present and of existence and impresses its seal on this knowledge: that existence is only an uninterrupted having-been, a thing which lives by denying itself, consuming itself, and contradicting itself.

If, in any sense, it is some happiness or the pursuit of happiness which binds the living being to life and urges him to live, then perhaps no philosopher is closer to the truth than the cynic: for the happiness of the animal, that thorough cynic, is the living proof of the truth of cynicism. The least happiness, if only it keeps one happy without interruption, is incomparably more than the greatest happiness which comes to one as a mere episode, as a mood, a frantic incursion into a life of utter displeasure, desire and privation. With the smallest as with the greatest happiness, however, there is always one thing which makes it happiness: being able to forget or, to express it in a more learned fashion, the capacity to live *unhistorically* while it endures. Whoever cannot settle on the threshold of the moment forgetful of the whole past, whoever is incapable of standing on a point like a goddess of victory without vertigo or fear, will never know what happiness is, and worse yet, will never do anything to make others happy. Take as an extreme example a man who possesses no trace of the power to forget, who is condemned everywhere to see becoming: such a one no longer believes in his own existence, no longer believes in himself; he sees everything flow apart in mobile points and loses himself in the stream of becoming: he will, like the true pupil of Heraclitus,[2] hardly

2. The allusion is to Cratylus who is said to have come to the view that, since no true statement can be made about a thing that is always changing, one ought not to say anything but only move one's finger. Cf. Aristotle, *Metaphysics*, 5, 1013 a13.

dare in the end to lift a finger. All acting requires forgetting, as not only light but also darkness is required for life by all organisms. A man who wanted to feel everything historically would resemble someone forced to refrain from sleeping, or an animal expected to live only from ruminating and ever repeated ruminating. So: it is possible to live with almost no memories, even to live happily as the animal shows; but without forgetting it is quite impossible to *live* at all. Or, to say it more simply yet: *there is a degree of insomnia, of rumination, of historical sense which injures every living thing and finally destroys it, be it a man, a people or a culture.*

To determine this degree, and through it the limit beyond which the past must be forgotten if it is not to become the gravedigger of the present, one would have to know precisely how great the *plastic power* of a man, a people or a culture is. I mean the power distinctively to grow out of itself, transforming and assimilating everything past and alien, to heal wounds, replace what is lost and reshape broken forms out of itself. There are men who have this power to so small a degree that they will incurably bleed to death over a single experience, a single pain, frequently over a single delicate injustice, as from quite a small bleeding laceration. On the other hand, there are those who are affected so little by the wildest and most gruesome calamities of life and even by their own malicious acts, that in midst of them or shortly thereafter they achieve a tolerable degree of well-being and a kind of clear conscience. The stronger the roots of the inmost nature of a man are, the more of the past will he appropriate or master; and were one to conceive the most powerful and colossal nature, it would be known by this, that for it there would be no limit at which the historical sense could overgrow and harm it; such a nature would draw its own as well as every alien past wholly into itself and transform it into blood, as it were. What such a nature cannot master it knows how to forget; it no longer exists, the horizon is closed and whole, and nothing can serve as a reminder that beyond this horizon there remain men, passions, doctrines and purposes. And this is a general law: every living thing can become healthy, strong and fruitful only within a horizon; if it is incapable of drawing a horizon around itself or, on the other hand, too selfish to restrict its vision to the limits of a horizon drawn by another, it will wither away feebly or overhastily to its early demise. Cheerfulness, clear conscience, the carefree deed, faith in the future, all this depends, in the case of an individual as well as of a people, on there being a line which distinguishes what is clear and in full view from the dark and unilluminable; it depends on one's being able to forget at the right time as well as to remember at the right time; on discerning with strong instinctual feelings when there is need to experience historically and when unhistorically. Precisely this is the proposition the reader is invited to consider: *the unhistorical and the historical are equally necessary for the health of an individual, a people and a culture.*

Everyone will have made the following observation: a man's historical
knowledge and perception may be very limited, his horizon as restricted as
that of a resident of an alpine valley, into every judgement he may in-
troduce an injustice, into every experience the error of being the first to
have that experience—and despite all injustice and all error he stands firm-
ly in indefatigable health and vigour, a pleasure to behold; while right
beside him the man of greater justice and learning deteriorates and
crumbles because the lines of his horizon restlessly shift again and again,
because he cannot extricate himself from the much more delicate network
of his justice and truths in order to engage in rude willing and desiring. We
have seen, however, that the animal, which is quite unhistorical and lives
within a horizon which is almost a point, nevertheless is in a certain sense
happy, or at least lives without boredom and dissimulation. We must then
consider the capacity to perceive unhistorically to a certain degree as the
more important and fundamental so far as it provides the foundation upon
which alone something right, healthy and great, something truly human
may grow. The unhistorical resembles an enveloping atmosphere in which
alone life is generated only to disappear again with the destruction of this
atmosphere. It is true: only so far as man, by thinking, reflecting, compar-
ing, dividing and joining, limits that unhistorical element; only so far as a
bright lightning flash of light occurs within that encircling cloud of
mist—that is, only through the power to use the past for life and to
refashion what has happened into history, does man become man: but
with an excess of history man ceases again, and without that cloak of the
unhistorical he would never have begun and dared to begin. Where are
there deeds which a man might have done without first having entered the
mist of the unhistorical? Or, leaving images aside, to illustrate with an example: think of a man tossed and torn by a powerful passion for a woman
or a great thought: how his world is changed! Glancing backwards he feels
blind, listening sideways he hears what is foreign as a dull meaningless
sound; what he perceives at all he has never perceived so before, so
tangibly near, coloured, full of sound and light as though he were ap-
prehending it with all his senses at once. All evaluations are changed and
devalued; there is so much he can no longer value because he can hardly
feel it: he asks himself whether he has been fooled the whole time by alien
words and alien opinions; he is astonished that his memory so tirelessly
runs in circles and is yet too weak and too tired to leap even once out of
this circle. It is the most unjust condition in the world, narrow, ungrateful
to the past, blind to dangers, deaf to warnings, a little living whirlpool in a
dead sea of night and forgetting: and yet this condition—unhistorical,
contra-historical through and through—is the cradle not only of an unjust,
but rather of every just deed; and no artist will paint his picture, no
general achieve victory nor any people its freedom without first having
desired and striven for it in such an unhistorical condition. As the man of

action, according to Goethe's[3] phrase, is always without conscience, so he is also without knowledge; he forgets a great deal to do one thing, he is unjust to what lies behind him and knows only one right, the right of that which is to become. So the agent loves his deed infinitely more than it deserves to be loved: and the best deeds occur in such an exuberance of love that of this love, at least, they must be unworthy even if their value is otherwise immeasurably great.

If someone could, in numerous instances, discern and breathe again the unhistorical atmosphere in which every great historical event came to be, then such a one might, as a cognitive being, perhaps elevate himself to a *superhistorical* standpoint such as Niebuhr[4] once described as the possible result of historical observation. "History", he says, "clearly and explicitly comprehended, has at least this one use: that one knows how even the greatest and highest spirits of humanity do not know how accidentally their vision adopted the form through which they see and through which they vehemently insist that everyone else see; vehemently that is, since the intensity of their consciousness is exceptionally great. Whoever does not know this and has not comprehended it quite definitely and in many instances will be subjugated by the appearance of a mighty spirit who brings the highest passion into a given form." One could call such a standpoint superhistorical, because one who has adopted it could no longer be tempted at all to continue to live and cooperate in making history, since he would have understood that blindness and injustice in the soul of each agent as the condition of all activity; he would even be cured henceforth of taking history excessively seriously: for he would have learned, with regard to each person and each experience, to answer his question about how and why people live, whether among Greeks or Turks, whether in an hour of the first century or the nineteenth. Whoever asks his acquaintances whether they would want to relive the last ten or twenty years will notice quite readily which of them is prepared for the superhistorical standpoint: they will, of course, all answer No!, but they will give different reasons for this No! The reason of some may be that they take comfort in the hope that the next twenty years will be better; it is they whom David Hume ridicules when he says:

> And from the dregs of life hope to receive,
> What the first sprightly running could not give.[5]

3. "The man of action is always without conscience; no one has a conscience except the observer." From "Sprüche in Prosa", quoted in *Gedanken aus Goethe's Werken,* ed. Hermann Levi, F. Bruckmann A.G., Munich, n.d. 4th edition, p. 80.

4. I believe that Barthold Georg Niebuhr is meant.

5. *Dialogues Concerning Natural Religion,* Part X, quoted with slight alteration from John Dryden, *Aureng-Zebe,* Act IV, Scene 1.

Let us call them the historical men. Looking into the past urges them toward the future, incites them to take courage and continue to engage in life, and kindles the hope that things will yet turn out well and that happiness is to be found behind the mountain toward which they are striding. These historical men believe that ever more light is shed on the meaning of existence in the course of its *process,* and they look back to consider that process only to understand the present better and learn to desire the future more vehemently. They do not know how unhistorically they think and act despite all their history, and how even their concern with historiography does not serve pure knowledge but life.

But the question whose first answer we have heard may also be answered differently. Of course again with a No!—but this time for different reasons. With the No of the superhistorical man who does not see salvation in the process, for whom, rather, the world is complete and achieves its end at every single moment. What could ten new years teach that the past ten were incapable of teaching!

Superhistorical men have never agreed whether the significance of the teaching is happiness or resignation, virtue or penance; but, opposed to all historical ways of viewing the past, they are quite unanimous in accepting the following proposition: the past and the present is one and the same, that is, typically alike in all manifold variety and, as omnipresence of imperishable types, a static structure of unchanged value and eternally the same meaning. As hundreds of different languages correspond to the typically fixed requirements of men, so that one who understood these requirements could learn nothing new from all those languages: so the superhistorical thinker illuminates all history of peoples and individuals from within, clairvoyantly guesses the original significance of the different hieroglyphs and gradually even evades, as one fatigued, the incessant flow of new script: how could he fail, amid the endless superfluity of events, to take in his fill, more than his fill, and finally be nauseated! So that in the end the boldest is perhaps prepared to say to his heart with Giacomo Leopardi:

> Nothing is worth
> One tremor or one beat; the very earth
> Deserves no sigh. Life
> Has shrunk to dregs and rancour; the world is unclean.
> Calm, calm.[6]

But let us leave the superhistorical men their nausea and their wisdom: today we want rather to rejoice in our unwisdom from the bottom of our hearts and as active and progressive men, as admirers of the process, enjoy

6. From Leopardi's poem "A se stesso" (To himself) translated by Edwin Morgan.

ourselves. May our estimation of the historical be but an occidental prejudice; as long as, within these prejudices, we make progress and do not stand still! As long as we constantly learn to improve our ability to do history for the sake of *life*. So long as we may always be sure of more life than they, we will gladly grant the superhistorical men that they have more wisdom: for in this way, at any rate, our unwisdom will have more of a future than their wisdom. And so that there may remain no doubt about the significance of this opposition between life and wisdom I shall call to aid a traditionally well proven procedure and straightway set up several theses.

A historical phenomenon clearly and completely understood and reduced to an intellectual phenomenon, is for him who has understood it dead: for in it he has understood the mania, the injustice, the blind passion, and in general the whole earthly darkened horizon of that phenomenon, and just in this he has understood its historical power. So far as he is a knower this power has now become powerless for him: not yet perhaps so far as he is a living being.

History, conceived as pure science and become sovereign, would constitute a kind of final closing out of the accounts of life for mankind. Historical education is wholesome and promising for the future only in the service of a powerful new life-giving influence, of a rising culture for example; that is, only when it is ruled and guided by a higher power and does not itself rule and guide.

History, so far as it serves life, serves an unhistorical power. While so subordinated it will and ought never, therefore, become a pure science like, say, mathematics. But the question to what degree life requires the service of history at all is one of the highest questions and concerns affecting the health of a man, a people, a culture. For with a certain excess of history life crumbles and degenerates, and finally, because of this degeneration, history itself degenerates as well.

2

That life requires the service of history, however, must be understood just as clearly as the proposition we intend to prove later—that an excess of history is detrimental to life. History belongs to the living man in three respects: it belongs to him so far as he is active and striving, so far as he preserves and admires, and so far as he suffers and is in need of liberation. To this triplicity of relations correspond three kinds of history: so far as they can be distinguished, a *monumental*, an *antiquarian* and a *critical* kind of history.

History belongs above all to the active and powerful man, to him who fights a great fight, who requires models, teachers and comforters and cannot find them among his associates and contemporaries. Thus history belonged to Schiller: for our age is so bad, says Goethe, that the poet encounters none to inspire him in the life that surrounds him. With respect to the man of action Polybius,[7] for example, calls political history the proper preparation for governing a state and the great teacher who, by reminding us of the sudden misfortunes of others, exhorts us steadfastly to bear the reverses of fortune. Whoever has learned to see the meaning of history in this must be distressed to see curious tourists or painstaking micrologists climbing around on the pyramids of monumental ages; where he has found incentive to do as others have done and do it better he does not want to meet the idler who, craving for distraction or sensation, strolls about as though among the heaped up pictorial treasures of some gallery. So as not to despair and be disgusted among frail and hopeless idlers, among contemporaries who appear to be active but in fact are merely wrought up and fidgetting, the man of action looks back and interrupts the course to his goal for once to breathe freely. His goal, however, is some happiness, perhaps not his own, often that of a people or of all mankind; he flees resignation and uses history as a means against resignation. In most cases, however, no reward beckons him unless it be fame, that is, the expectation of a place of honour in the temple of history where he himself may teach, console, and warn those who come after him. For his commandment reads: what once was capable of magnifying the concept 'man' and of giving it a more beautiful content must be present eternally in order eternally to have this capacity. That the great moments in the struggle of individuals form a chain, that in them the high points of humanity are linked throughout millennia, that what is highest in such a moment of the distant past be for me still alive, bright and great—this is the fundamental thought of the faith in humanity which is expressed in the demand for a *monumental* history. Precisely this demand however, that the great be eternal, occasions the most terrible conflict. For all else which also lives cries no. The monumental ought not arise—that is the counterwatch-word. Dull habit, the small and lowly which fills all corners of the world and wafts like a dense earthly vapour around everything great, deceiving, smothering and suffocating, obstructs the path which the great must still travel to immortality. Yet this path leads through human brains! Through the brains of frightened shortlived animals who repeatedly rise to the same needs and with effort fend off their destruction for a short time. For above all they want one thing: to live at all cost. Who could suspect in them the arduous torch race of monumental history through which alone the great lives on! And yet time and again some awaken who, in viewing past greatness and strengthened by their vision, rejoice as though human life were a grand affair and as though it were even the sweetest fruit of this bitter growth to know that at some earlier time someone went through ex-

7. *The Histories*, trans. W. R. Paton, Harvard University Press and William Heinemann Ltd., London, 1967, Vol. I, p. 3.

istence proud and strong, another in profound thought, a third helpfully and with pity—yet all leaving one lesson, that he lives most splendidly who pays no heed to existence. If the common man views this span of time with such sad seriousness and finds it so desirable, then these others, on their way to immortality and monumental history, knew how to disregard it with Olympian laughter or at least with lofty scorn; they often went to their graves with irony—for what did they have that could be buried! Surely no more than what had always oppressed them as dross, excrement, vanity and animality which will now fall into forgetfulness after it had long been given over to their contempt. But one thing will live, the monogram of their most authentic essence, a work, a deed, a rare inspiration, a creation: it will live because posterity cannot do without it. In this most refined form fame is more than the most delicious morsel of our self-love, as Schopenhauer[8] called it; it is the belief in the affinity and continuity of the great of all ages, it is a protest against the change of generations and transitoriness.

What is the advantage to the present individual, then, of the monumental view of the past, the concern with the classical and the rare of earlier times? It is the knowledge that the great which once existed was at least *possible* once and may well again be possible sometime; he goes his way more courageously, for now the doubt which assails him in moments of weakness, that he may perhaps want the impossible, has been conquered. Suppose someone were to believe that it required no more than a hundred productive men, raised and active in a new spirit, to put an end to the cultural refinement which has just now become fashionable in Germany, how it would strengthen him to realize that the culture of the Renaissance was raised on the shoulders of such a group of one hundred men.

And yet—at once to learn another new thing from the same example—how flowing and elusive, how imprecise would such a comparison be! How much that is different must be overlooked, how ruthlessly must the individuality of the past be forced into a general form and have all its sharp edges and lines broken for the sake of agreement, if the comparison is to have that powerful effect! Fundamentally what was possible once could only be possible a second time if the Pythagoreans were right in believing that with the same conjunction of the heavenly bodies the same events had to be repeated on earth down to the minutest detail: so that whenever the stars have a certain relation to each other a Stoic will join with an Epicurean and murder Caesar, and ever again with a different configuration Columbus will discover America. Only if the earth again and again began her drama anew after the fifth act, if it were certain that the

8. "Considered eudaemonistically, then, fame is nothing more than the rarest and most delicious morsel for our pride and our vanity." Arthur Schopenhauer, *Sämtliche Werke*, ed. Wolfgang Freiherr von Löhneisen, Wissenschaftliche Buchgesellschaft, Darmstadt, 1968, Vol. IV, p. 475.

same tangle of motives, the same *deus ex machina,* the same catastrophe recurred at definite intervals, should the powerful man desire monumental history in complete pictorial *truthfulness,* that is, desire each fact in its precisely depicted character and uniqueness: thus probably not before the astronomers become astrologers again. Until then monumental history will not find such complete truthfulness to its advantage: it will always approximate, generalize and finally equate differences; it will always weaken the disparity of motives and occasions in order, at the expense of the *cause,* to present the *effect* monumentally, that is, as exemplary and worthy of imitation. Monumental history then, since it disregards causes as much as possible, could without much exaggeration be called a collection of "effects in themselves", or of events which will at all times produce an effect. What is celebrated in national festivals and in religious or military days of remembrance is actually such an "effect in itself": it is this which gives no rest to the ambitious, which the enterprising take to heart like an amulet, and not the true, historical nexus of causes and effects which, if fully understood, would only prove that never again could quite the same thing result in the game of dice played by chance and the future.

As long as the soul of historiography is found in the great incentives a powerful man receives from it, as long as the past must be described as something worthy of imitation, something that can be imitated and is possible a second time, so long, at least, is the past in danger of being somewhat distorted, of being reinterpreted according to aesthetic criteria and so brought closer to fiction; there are even ages which are quite incapable of distinguishing between a monumental past and a mythical fiction: for precisely the same incentives can be given by the one world as by the other. Thus, whenever the monumental vision of the past *rules* over the other ways of looking at the past, I mean the antiquarian and the critical, the past itself suffers *damage:* very great portions of the past are forgotten and despised, and flow away like a grey uninterrupted flood, and only single embellished facts stand out as islands: there seems to be something unnatural and wondrous about the rare persons who become visible at all, like the golden hip which the pupils of Pythagoras thought they discerned in their master. Monumental history deceives with analogies: with tempting similarities the courageous are enticed to rashness, the enthusiastic to fanaticism; and if one thinks of this history as being in the hands and heads of talented egoists and enraptured rascals then empires are destroyed, princes murdered, wars and revolutions instigated and the number of historical "effects in themselves," that is, of effects without sufficient causes, is further increased. So much as a reminder of the damage which monumental history can cause among the mighty and active, be they good or evil: but what can it not inflict if the impotent and inactive master it and put it to their uses!

Let us take the simplest and most frequent example. Think of artless and feebly artistic natures girded and armed by monumental history of art and artists: against whom will they now direct their weapons? Against their traditional enemies, the strong artistic spirits, namely against those who alone are capable of learning truly, that is, for the sake of life, from that history and of putting what they have learned into higher practice. It is their path which is obstructed and their air which is darkened when one dances idolatrously and diligently round a half understood monument of some great past, as though to say: "See, this is true and real art: what do you care about aspiring newcomers!" Apparently this dancing swarm even has a monopoly on "good taste": for the creator has always been at a disadvantage to him who only looked on without even trying his hand; as at all times the armchair politician has been wiser, more just and judicious than the governing statesman. If, however, the use of the popular vote and numerical majorities were transferred to the realm of art and the artist required to defend himself before a forum of the aesthetically inactive, you may bet your life that he would be condemned: not despite, but just *because* of the fact that his judges have solemnly proclaimed the canon of monumental art (that is, according to the given explanation, of art which has at all times "produced an effect"). While for all art which is not yet monumental because still contemporary they lack first, any need, second, any genuine inclination, third, just that authority of history. On the other hand their instinct tells them that art may be beaten to death with art: the monumental must definitely not be produced again, and what happens to have the authority of monumentality from the past is just the right preventative. This is how the connoisseurs are because they wish to eliminate art altogether; they give the appearance of physicians while their real intention is to dispense poisons; so they cultivate their tongue and their taste in order to explain fastidiously why they so insistently decline whatever nourishing artistic fare is offered them. For they do not want something great to be produced: their expedient is to say "see, the great already exists!" In truth they care as little about existing greatness as about greatness in the making: to that their life bears witness. Monumental history is the disguise in which their hatred of the mighty and the great of their time parades as satisfied admiration of the mighty and the great of past ages. Cloaked in this disguise they turn the proper sense of monumental history into its opposite; whether they know it clearly or not, at any rate they act as though their motto were: let the dead bury the living.

Each of the three kinds of history is justified in only one soil and one climate: in every other it grows into a noxious weed. If the man who wants to achieve something great needs the past at all he will master it through monumental history; who on the other hand likes to persist in the traditional and venerable will care for the past as an antiquarian historian; and only he who is oppressed by some present misery and wants to throw off the burden at all cost has a need for critical, that is judging and condemning history. Much harm is caused by thoughtless transplanting: the critic without need, the antiquarian without reverence, the connoisseur of the great who has not the ability to achieve the great are such growths which have been alienated from their native soil and therefore have degenerated and shot up as weeds.

3

In the second place, then, history belongs to the preserving and revering soul—to him who with loyalty and love looks back on his origins; through this reverence he, as it were, gives thanks for his existence. By tending with loving hands what has long survived he intends to preserve the conditions in which he grew up for those who will come after him—and so he serves life. The possession of ancestral furniture changes its meaning in such a soul: for the soul is rather possessed by the furniture. The small and limited, the decayed and obsolete receives its dignity and inviolability in that the preserving and revering soul of the antiquarian moves into these things and makes itself at home in the nest it builds there. The history of his city becomes for him the history of his self; he understands the wall, the turreted gate, the ordinance of the town council, the national festival like an illustrated diary of his youth and finds himself, his strength, his diligence, his pleasure, his judgment, his folly and rudeness, in all of them. Here one could live, he says to himself, for here one can live and will be able to live, for we are tough and not to be uprooted over night. And so, with this "We", he looks beyond the ephemeral, curious, individual life and feels like the spirit of the house, the generation, and the city. Occasionally he will greet the soul of his people as his own soul even across the wide, obscuring and confusing centuries; and power of empathy and divination, of scenting an almost cold trail, of instinctively reading aright the past however much it be written over, a quick understanding of the palimpsests, even polypsests—these are his gifts and virtues. With them Goethe stood before the memorial of Erwin von Steinbach; in the tempest of his emotions the historical cloudcover spread between them tore, and for the first time he saw the German work again "exerting its influence out of a strong robust German soul".[9] Such a sense and disposition guided the Italians of the Renaissance and reawakened in their poets the ancient Italic genius to a "wondrous reverberation of the ancient lyre", [10] as Jakob Burckhardt puts it. But this antiquarian historical sense of reverence is of highest value where it imbues modest, coarse, even wretched conditions in

9. The reference is to Goethe's essay "Von deutscher Baukunst" which is dedicated to the departed spirit (*divis manibus*) of Erwin von Steinbach. The quotation is found near the end of this short essay.

10. Jacob Burckhardt, *Die Cultur der Renaissance in Italien*, 4th edition, Leipzig, 1885, Vol. I, p. 286.

which a man or a people live with a simple touching feeling of pleasure and contentment; as for example Niebuhr honestly and candidly admits to living cheerfully on moor and heath among free peasants who have a history, without ever missing art. How could history serve life better than by tying even less favoured generations and populations to their homeland and its customs, by making them sedentary and preventing their searching and contentiously fighting for something better in foreign lands? At times what, as it were, nails an individual down to these companions and environment, to this tiresome habit, to this bare mountaintop seems to be stubbornness and unreason—but it is a most wholesome unreason productive of the common goal: as everyone knows who is aware of the terrible consequences of an adventurous urge to emigrate, say, in whole hordes of populations, or who closely observes the condition of a people which has lost its loyalty to its earlier times and is given over to a restless cosmopolitan choosing and searching for novelty and ever more novelty. The opposite sentiment, the contentment of a tree with its roots, the happiness of knowing oneself not to be wholly arbitrary and accidental, but rather as growing out of a past as its heir, flower and fruit and so to be exculpated, even justified, in one's existence—this is what one now especially likes to call the proper historical sense.

These, of course, are not the conditions which most favour a man's ability to reduce the past to pure knowledge; and we see again here what we have seen in the case of monumental history, that the past itself suffers as long as history serves life and is ruled by the impulses of life. To use a somewhat stretched metaphor: the tree feels its roots more than it can see them; this feeling, however, measures their size by the size and strength of its visible branches. The tree may already be in error here: but how much greater will its error be about the whole forest which surrounds it! of which it only knows and feels anything so far as it is hindered or helped by it—but nothing beyond that. The antiquarian sense of a man, of an urban community, of a whole people always has an extremely limited field of vision; by far the most is not seen at all, and the little that is seen is seen too closely and in isolation; it cannot apply a standard and therefore takes everything to be equally important and therefore each individual thing to be too important. Under these circumstances there are no differences in value and no proportions for the things of the past which would truly do justice to those things in relation to each other; but only measures and proportions of those things in relation to the antiquarian individual or people looking back at them.

Here there is always one danger very near: the time will finally come when everything old and past which has not totally been lost sight of will simply be taken as equally venerable, while whatever does not approach the old with veneration, that is, the new and growing, will be rejected and treated with hostility. Thus even the Greeks tolerated the hieratic style of their plastic arts beside a freer and greater style; and later not only tolerated the pointed noses and frosty smiles but even made of them a matter of refinement in artistic taste. When the sense of a people hardens in this way, when history serves past life so as to undermine further and especially higher life, when the historical sense no longer preserves life but mummifies it: then the tree dies unnaturally, beginning at the top and slowly dying toward the roots—and in the end the root itself generally decays. Antiquarian history itself degenerates the moment that the fresh life of the present no longer animates and inspires it. Now piety withers away, scholarly habit endures without it and, egoistically complacent, revolves around its own centre. Then you may well witness the repugnant spectacle of a blind lust for collecting, of a restless raking together of all that once has been. Man envelops himself in an odour of decay; through his antiquarian habit he succeeds in degrading even a more significant talent and nobler need to an insatiable craving for novelty, or rather a craving for all things and old things; often he sinks so low as finally to be satisfied with any fare and devours with pleasure even the dust of bibliographical quisquilia.

But even if that degeneration does not come about, if antiquarian history does not lose the foundation in which alone it can take root for the benefit of life: there are always left dangers enough should it become too powerful and overgrow the other ways of seeing the past. It merely understands how to *preserve* life, not how to generate it; therefore it always underestimates what is in process of becoming because it has no instinct for discerning its significance—unlike monumental history, for example, which has this instinct. Thus it hinders the powerful resolve for new life, thus it paralyzes the man of action who, as man of action, will and must always injure some piety or other. The fact that something has become old now gives rise to the demand that it must be immortal; for if one calculates what such an ancient thing—an old ancestral custom, a religious faith, an inherited political privilege—has experienced during its existence, the amount of piety and veneration paid by individuals and generations: then it seems presumptuous or even impious to replace such an ancient thing with a new one and to compare such a vast sum of acts of piety and veneration with the single-digit numbers of what is becoming and present.

Here it becomes clear how badly man needs, often enough, in addition to the monumental and antiquarian ways of seeing the past, a *third* kind, the *critical*: and this again in the service of life as well. He must have the strength, and use it from time to time, to shatter and dissolve something to enable him to live: this he achieves by dragging it to the bar of judgment, interrogating it meticulously and finally condemning it; every past, however, is worth condemning—for that is how matters happen to stand with human affairs: human violence and weakness have always contributed strongly to shaping them. It is not justice which here sits in judgment; even less is it mercy which here pronounces judgment: but life alone, that dark, driving, insatiably self-desiring power. Its verdict is always unmerciful, always unjust, because it has never flowed from a pure fountain of knowledge; but in most cases the verdict would be the same were justice itself to proclaim it. For "whatever has a beginning *deserves* to have an undoing; it would be better if nothing began at all."[11] It takes a great deal of strength to be able to live and to forget how far living and being unjust are one. Luther himself once thought that the world came to be through an oversight of God: for had God thought of "heavy artillery" he would never have created the world. Occasionally, however, the same life which needs forgetfulness demands the temporary destruction of this forgetfulness; then it is to become clear how unjust is the existence of some thing, a privilege, a caste, a dynasty for example, how much this thing deserves destruction. Then its past is considered critically, then one puts the knife to its roots, then one cruelly treads all pieties under foot. It is always a dangerous process, namely dangerous for life itself: and men or ages which serve life in this manner of judging and annihilating a past are always dangerous and endangered men and ages. For since we happen to be the results of earlier generations we are also the results of their aberrations, passions and errors, even crimes; it is not possible quite to free oneself from this chain. If we condemn those aberrations and think ourselves quite exempt from them, the fact that we are descended from them is not eliminated. At best we may bring about a conflict between our inherited, innate nature and our knowledge, as well as a battle between a strict new discipline and ancient education and breeding; we implant a new habit, a new instinct, a second nature so that the first nature withers away. It is an attempt, as it were, *a posteriori* to give oneself a past from which one would like to be descended in opposition to the past from which one is descended:—always a dangerous attempt because it is so difficult to find a limit in denying the past and because second natures are mostly feebler than the first. Too often we stop at knowing the good without doing it because we also know the better without being able to do it. Yet here and there a victory is achieved nevertheless, and for the fighters who use critical history for life there is even a remarkable consolation: namely, to know that this first nature also was, at some time or other, a second nature and that every victorious second nature becomes a first.

4

These are the services which history is capable of rendering to life; each

11. J. W. von Goethe, *Faust,* Part I. The lines are spoken by Mephistopheles in the early scene in Faust's study. We quote the translation by Louis MacNeice and E. L. Stahl.

man and each people requires, according to their goals, strengths and needs, a certain knowledge of the past, sometimes as monumental, sometimes as antiquarian, sometimes as critical history: but not like a crowd of pure thinkers who only contemplate life, not like individuals, hungry for knowledge, satisfied with mere knowledge, whose only goal is the increase of knowledge, but always only for the purpose of life and therefore also always under the rule and highest direction of that purpose. That this is the natural relation of an age, a culture, a people to history—brought on by hunger, regulated by the degree of need, held within limits by the inherent plastic power—that knowledge of the past is at all times desired only in the service of the future and the present, not to weaken the present, not to uproot a future strong with life: all of this is simple, as truth is simple, and immediately convinces even him who has not first been given a historical proof.

And now a quick glance at our time! We are shocked, we fly back: whither is all clarity, all naturalness and purity of that relation between life and history, how confused, how exaggerated, how troubled is this problem which now surges before our eyes! Is the fault ours, the observers? Or has the constellation of life and history really changed because a powerful, hostile star has come between them? May others show that we have seen falsely: we will say what we believe we see. Such a star has indeed intervened, a bright and glorious star, the constellation is really changed—*through science, through the demand that history be a science.* Now life is no longer the sole ruler and master of knowledge of the past: rather all boundary markers are overthrown and everything which once was rushes in upon man. All perspectives have shifted as far back as the origins of change, back into infinity. A boundless spectacle such as history, the science of universal becoming, now displays, no generation has ever seen; of course, she displays it with the dangerous boldness of her motto: *fiat veritas pereat vita.*[12]

Let us now picture to ourselves the spiritual events brought on hereby in the soul of modern man. Historical knowledge floods in ever anew from inexhaustible springs, the alien and disconnected throngs about, memory opens all its gates and is still not opened wide enough, nature makes a supreme effort to receive these alien guests, to order and to honour them, but these themselves are at war with each other and it appears necessary to master and overcome them all so as not oneself to perish in their strife. Gradually it becomes second nature to get accustomed to such a disorderly, stormy, belligerent household, while at the same time it is beyond question that this second nature is much weaker, much more troubled and through and through less healthy than the first.

12. Let there be truth, and may life perish.

In the end modern man drags an immense amount of indigestible knowledge stones around with him which on occasion rattle around in his belly, as the fairy tale[13] has it. This rattling betrays the most distinctive property of this modern man: the remarkable opposition of an inside to which no outside and an outside to which no inside corresponds, an opposition unknown to ancient peoples. Knowledge, taken in excess without hunger, even contrary to need, no longer acts as a transforming motive impelling to action and remains hidden in a certain chaotic inner world which that modern man, with curious pride, calls his unique "inwardness". He may then say that he has the content and that only the form is lacking; but in all living things this is quite an unseemly opposition. Our modern culture is nothing living just because it cannot be understood at all without that opposition, that is: it is no real culture at all, but only a kind of knowledge about culture, it stops at cultured thoughts and cultured feelings but leads to no cultured decisions. That, however, which truly is a motive and visibly shows itself in action often signifies little more than an indifferent convention, a miserable imitation or even a rude grimace. In the inner being sentiment may well sleep like the snake which, having swallowed whole rabbits, calmly lies in the sun and avoids all movement except the most necessary. The inner process, that is now the thing itself, that is properly "culture". Everyone who passes by wishes only one thing, that such a culture not perish of indigestibility. Think, for example, of a Greek passing by such a culture, he would perceive that for more recent men 'educated' and 'historically educated' appear to belong together as though they were one and distinguished only by the number of words. Were he now to give voice to his tenet: a man can be very educated and yet be historically quite uneducated, one would believe not to have heard properly and shake one's head. That well known little people of a not too distant past, I mean just the Greeks, had stubbornly preserved its unhistorical sense in the period of its greatest strength; were a contemporary man forced by magic spells to return to that world he would presumably find the Greeks very "uneducated", which would, of course, disclose the meticulously disguised secret of modern culture to public laughter: for from ourselves we moderns have nothing at all; only by filling and overfilling ourselves with alien ages, customs, arts, philosophies, religions and knowledge do we become something worthy of notice, namely walking encyclopedias, as which an ancient Hellene, who had been thrown into our age, might perhaps address us. The whole value of encyclopedias, however, is found only in what is written in them, the content, not in what is written on them or in what is cover and what is shell; and so the whole of modern culture is essentially internal: on the outside the bookbinder has printed something like "Handbook of Inner Culture for Exter-

13. Little Red Riding Hood

nal Barbarians". This opposition of inside and outside makes the outside still more barbaric than it would need to be were a rude people to grow out of itself alone according to its rough requirements. For what means is left to nature to take in what imposes itself so excessively? Only the one means, to accept it as easily as possible in order quickly to lay it aside again and expel it. This gives rise to a habit of not taking actual things too seriously anymore, this gives rise to the "weak personality" as a result of which the actual and enduring make only a minimal impression; in externals one finally becomes ever more casual and indolent and widens the critical gulf between content and form to the point of insensitivity to barbarism, if only the memory is stimulated ever anew, if only ever new things to be known keep streaming in to be neatly put on display in the cases of that memory. The culture of a people in contrast to that barbarism has once been designated, with some justification I believe, as unity of artistic style in all expressions of life of a people;[14] this designation should not be misunderstood as though the opposition between barbarism and *beautiful* style were at issue; the people that can be called cultured must in reality be a living unity and not fall apart so miserably into an inside and an outside, a content and a form. If you want to strive for and promote the culture of a people, then strive for and promote this higher unity and work to annihilate modern pseudo-culture in favour of a true culture; dare to devote some thought to the problem of restoring the health of a people which has been impaired by history, to how it may recover its instincts and therewith its integrity.

I wish only to speak plainly of us Germans of the present, of us who suffer more than another people from that weakness of personality and the contradiction of content and form. Form is for us Germans generally a convention, a costume and disguise, and for that reason it is, if not hated, at least not loved; it would be more correct still to say that we are extraordinarily afraid of the word 'convention', and surely also of the thing 'convention'. With this fear the German left the school of the French: for he wanted to become more natural and thereby more German. However, he seems to have miscalculated this 'thereby': having run away from the school of convention he let himself go as and where it pleased him, and basically imitated sloppily and arbitrarily in partial forgetfulness what earlier he imitated meticulously and often successfully. Even today we still live, compared with earlier times, by slovenly, incorrect French convention: as all our walking, standing, conversation, dress and home life shows. We thought we had come back to being natural; but we merely chose to let ourselves go, we chose indolent comfort and the smallest possible degree of self-control. Walk around any German city—all convention, compared with the national character of foreign

14. This probably refers to the first of Nietzsche's Untimely Observations, *David Strauß*.

cities, will prove to be negative, all is colourless, worn down, badly copied, careless, each man follows his fancy, but not a strong thoughtful fancy, rather according to laws prescribed at one time by general haste and at another by the general craving for comfort. A piece of clothing whose invention requires no great mental effort, which takes no time to put on, that is, a piece of clothing borrowed from foreigners and copied as carelessly as possible, counts with Germans at once as a contribution to German fashion. The sense of form is rejected by them with veritable irony—one has, after all, *the sense of content:* they are, after all, the famous people of inwardness.

There is, however, a famous danger in this inwardness: the content itself, of which it is assumed that it cannot be seen at all from the outside, may at some time or other evaporate; externally one would not detect a trace of this nor of its earlier presence. But however far one may believe the German people to be from this danger: the foreigner will never be quite wrong in his reproach that our inner being is too weak and disorderly to have an external effect and give itself a form. Yet it may prove to be delicately receptive to a rare degree, serious, powerful, fervent, good and perhaps even richer than the inner being of other peoples: but as a whole it remains weak, since all those beautiful fibres are not entwined into a strong knot: so that the visible deed is not the deed of the whole and a self-manifestation of this inner being, but only a feeble and rude attempt of some fibre or other wanting for the sake of appearance to count as the whole. Therefore the German cannot be judged at all by an action and remains hidden as an individual even after this deed. He must, as is well known, be measured by his thoughts and his feelings and these he now expresses in his books. If only it were not just these books which lately raise more than a doubt, whether this famous inwardness still sits in its inaccessible little temple: it would be terrible to think that it disappeared one day and all that now remains as the distinguishing mark of the German is his outer being, that arrogantly clumsy and meekly ineffectual outer being. It would be almost as terrible as if that inwardness were to sit in there hidden from view, a counterfeit rouged and painted, having become an actress if not something worse: as for example Grillparzer, standing aside and calmly observing, seems to have come to believe through his dramatic-theatrical experience. "We feel with abstraction", he says, "we hardly know any longer how feeling is expressed by our contemporaries; we portray expressions of feeling which no longer occur nowadays. Shakespeare has spoiled all of us moderns."[15]

This is a single case perhaps too quickly interpreted as holding general-

15. Grillparzer F., *Werke*, Der Tempel-Verlag, Berlin and Darmstadt, 1965, Vol. II, pp. 285-6.

ly: but how terrible would be its justified generalization, if all too many single cases imposed themselves on the observer, what despair would ring in this proposition: we Germans feel with abstraction; we have all been spoiled by history—a proposition which would destroy at its roots all hope of a national culture still to come: for every hope of this kind is nourished by the belief in the genuineness and immediacy of German feeling, by the belief in an unharmed inwardness. What is there still to be hoped and believed when the spring of belief and hope is muddied, when inwardness has learned to leap, to dance, to use make-up, to express itself with abstraction and calculation and gradually to lose itself! And how shall the great productive spirit still find it tolerable to remain with a people which is no longer sure of its unifying inwardness and which falls apart into the educated with a miseducated and misguided inwardness and the uneducated with an inaccessible inwardness. How can this spirit tolerate it if the integrity of a people's feeling is lost, if moreover he finds this feeling a rouged counterfeit in just that part which calls itself the educated part of the people and claims a right to the national artistic spirits. Even if here and there the judgment and taste of individuals had grown finer and more refined—that does not compensate this spirit; he is tormented by having to speak only to a sect, as it were, and no longer being necessary in the midst of his people. Perhaps he would rather bury his treasure now because he feels revulsion at being pretentiously patronized by a sect while his heart is filled with pity for all. The instinct of the people no longer goes out to him; it is useless to long for him with open arms. What else is left to him but to turn his inspired hatred towards that hindering constraint, against the barriers erected by the so-called education of his people, to condemn as judge what for him who lives and generates life is annihilation and degradation: so he exchanges the deep insight of his fate for the divine pleasure of creating and helping and ends in lonely knowledge as a surfeited sage. It is the most painful spectacle: whoever sees it at all will discern a holy demand here: he says to himself, one must help here, that higher unity in the nature and soul of a people must be remade, that break between the inside and the outside must disappear under the hammer blows of need. What means shall he use? What is now left him but his deep knowledge: in expressing it, disseminating it, distributing it generously he hopes to plant a need: and from this strong need a strong deed will one day arise. And so as to leave no doubt from where I take the example of that need, that want, that knowledge: I shall explicitly set down my testimony here that it is *German unity* in that highest sense for which we strive and strive for more ardently than political reunification, the *unity of the German spirit and life after the annihilation of the opposition of form and content, of inwardness and convention.*

5

The surfeit of history of an age seems to me hostile and dangerous to life in five respects: through such an excess the contrast of inside and outside, discussed above, is generated and the personality weakened thereby; through this excess an age comes to imagine that it possesses the rarest virtue, justice, to a higher degree than any other age; through this excess the instincts of a people are impaired and the maturing of the individual no less than of the whole is prevented; through this excess the belief, harmful at any time, in the old age of mankind is implanted, the belief of being a latecomer and epigone; through this excess an age acquires the dangerous disposition of irony with regard to itself, and from this the still more dangerous one of cynicism: in this, however, it ripens even more into clever egoistic practice through which the vital strength is paralized and finally destroyed.

And now back to our first proposition: modern man suffers from a weakened personality. As the Roman of the Empire ceased to be Roman with regard to the region of the world which was at his service, as he lost himself in the influx of the foreign and degenerated in the cosmopolitan carnival of gods, customs, and arts, so it must go with modern man who continuously has the feast of a world exhibition prepared for him by his historical artists; he has become a spectator merely enjoying himself and strolling around and brought to a condition which can hardly be altered for a moment even by great wars and great revolutions. The war is not yet over and already it has been transformed a hundred thousandfold into printed paper, already it is being served up as a new stimulant for the weary palates of those greedy for history. It appears almost impossible to elicit a strong full sound even with the mightiest sweep of the strings: it fades away immediately, and in the next moment it already echoes away strengthless in historically subdued vapours. In moral language: you no longer succeed in holding fast the sublime, your deeds are sudden claps, not rolling thunder. Achieve the greatest and most wonderful: it must nevertheless go to Orcus unsung. For art flees if you immediately spread the historical awning over your deeds. Whoever wants to understand, calculate, comprehend in a moment where with profoundly sustained emotion he ought to hold fast the unintelligible as the sublime, may be called rational, but only in the sense in which Schiller speaks of the reason of reasonable men: he fails to see something which is yet seen by the child, he fails to hear something which is yet heard by the child; this something is exactly the most important: because he does not understand this his understanding is more childish than the child and simpler than simplicity— despite the many clever wrinkles on his parchment face and the masterly skill his fingers have in unraveling tangles. It comes to this: he has annihilated and lost his instinct; when his reason wavers and his way leads through deserts he can no longer let go the reins and trust in the "divine animal". So the individual becomes timid and unsure and may no longer believe in himself: he sinks into himself, into his inner being, which here only means: into the heaped up chaos of knowledge which fails to have an external effect, of teaching which does not become life. If we regard their outside we notice how the expulsion of the instincts by history has almost transformed men into downright *abstractis* and shadows: no one dares to show his person, but masks himself as an educated man, as a scholar, a poet, a politician. If one takes hold of such masks believing them to be real and not just a puppet show—for they all pretend to be real—one suddenly has hold of nothing but rags and multi-coloured patches. Therefore one ought no longer to allow oneself to be deceived, therefore one ought to address them imperiously: "take off your jackets or be what you seem!" No longer shall everyone who is serious by nature become a Don Quixote, for they have better things to do than fight with such presumed realities. At least each ought to look closely, call his "Halt! Who goes there?" to each mask and tear it off. How strange! One should think that history would, above all, encourage men to be *honest*—even if it were to be an honest fool; and it has always had this effect, but no longer! Historical education and the universal frock of the citizen rule at the same time. While there has never been such sonorous talk of the "free personality" one does not even see personalities, not to speak of free ones, rather nothing but timidly disguised universal men. The individual has withdrawn into his inner being: externally one discerns nothing of him anymore; whereby one may doubt whether there can be any causes without effects. Or is a race of eunuchs required to guard the great historical world-harem? Pure objectivity is most becoming in such men, of course. It almost seems as though the task were to guard history so that nothing could come of it but stories, but by no means history-making events!—to prevent its making personalities "free", that is, sincere toward themselves, sincere towards others, and that in word and deed. Only through this sincerity will the distress, the inner misery of modern man reach the light of day and the timidly hidden convention and masquerade can then be replaced by art and religion as true helpers, together to plant a culture which is adequate to true needs and not, like contemporary general education, only teach to lie to oneself about these needs and thus to become a walking lie.

In how unnatural, artificial, in any case unworthy a condition must the most sincere of all the sciences, the honest naked goddess philosophy, find herself in an age which suffers from general education! In such a world of forced external uniformity she remains a learned monologue of the lonely walker, the chance prey of the solitary thinker, a hidden private secret or harmless gossip of academic old men and children. No one may dare to fulfill the law of philosophy in himself, no one lives philosophically, with that simple manful constancy which compelled one of the ancients, wherever he was, whatever he was doing, to behave like a Stoic if once he had pledged allegiance to the Stoa. All modern philosophizing is political and official, limited to learned appearance by governments, churches, academies, customs, and the cowardices of men; it stops with the sigh "if only" or with the realization "once upon a time". Philosophy has no rights within historical education if it wants to be more than an inwardly restrained knowing without effect; if modern man were only courageous and resolute, if only he were not only an inward being even in his enmities: he would banish philosophy; but as it is he is satisfied with modestly draping her nakedness. One does think, write, print, teach philosophically—all of this is more or less permitted; only in action, in so-called life all is different: only one thing is permitted here and everything else simply impossible: so historical education wills it. Are these still human beings, one then asks oneself, or only machines that think, write and talk?

Goethe once said of Shakespeare: "No one despised the material costume more than he; he knows the inner human costume very well, and here all are alike. It is said that he portrayed the Romans very well; I do not think so, they are all inveterate Englishmen, but, of course, they are men, men from top to bottom, and assuredly the Roman toga fits them."[16] Now I ask whether it would be at all possible to present our contemporary literati, popular men, officials, politicians as Romans; it would be quite impossible because they are not men but only incarnate compendia and, as it were, concrete abstractions. If they have character and a manner of their own, then all this is seated so deeply that it cannot struggle out to the light of day at all: if they are men they can be known as such only by one who plumbs them deeply. For all others they are something else, not men, not gods, not animals, but historically educated patterns, through and through formation, image, form without demonstrable content, unfortunately only bad form, and moreover uniform. And so my proposition may be taken and understood: *only strong personalities can endure history; the weak are completely extinguished by it.* The reason is that history confuses feeling and sentiment where these are not strong enough to make themselves the measure of the past. The man who no longer dares to trust himself, but, seeking counsel from history about his feelings, asks "how am I to feel here", will, from timidity, gradually become an actor and play a role, mostly even many roles and therefore each so badly and superficially. Gradually all congruence between the man and his historical scope is lost; we see cheeky little fellows treating the Romans as though they were their equals: and they dig and burrow in the remains of Greek

16. J. W. von Goethe, "Shakespeare und kein Ende". The quotation is near the beginning of this essay.

poets as though even these *corpora*[17] lay prepared for their dissection and were *vilia*, which their own literary *corpora* may be. Let us assume a man working on Democritis; I always have the question at the tip of my tongue: why not Heraclitus? Or Philo? Or Bacon? Or Descartes?—and so on at random. And then: just why a philosopher? Why not a poet, an orator? And: why especially a Greek, why not an Englishman, a Turk? Is not the past large enough to find something that will not make even you appear so ridiculously arbitrary? But, as I have said, it is a race of eunuchs; one woman is like the next to the eunuch, just a woman, woman in itself, the eternally unapproachable—and so it is a matter of indifference what you do as long as history itself is preserved nice and "objective", namely by those who can never themselves make history. And since the eternally feminine will never draw you up to itself,[18] you draw it down to you and, as neuters, take history to be a neuter as well. Lest one believe, however, that I seriously compare history with the eternal feminine, I shall rather clearly state that, on the contrary, I take it to be the eternal masculine: only that for those who are "historically educated" through and through it cannot matter very much whether it is one or the other: after all, they are themselves neither man nor woman, not even hermaphrodites, but always only neuters, or, to use a more educated expression, only the eternally objective ones.

Once personalities are drained, in the manner described, to the point of eternal non-subjectivity, or, as one says, objectivity: nothing can affect them any longer; should something good and right happen, as deed, as poetry, as music: at once those hollowed out by education will look beyond the work and inquire after the history of the author. If he has already produced several other works, he must at once suffer to have the past and projected future direction of his development explained to him, at once he is held up beside others for comparison, with regard to the choice and treatment of his material he will be dissected, torn apart, wisely put back together and on the whole admonished and reprimanded. Something most astonishing may happen, the flock of historical neuters is always already on the spot, prepared to comprehend the author from afar. Momentarily the echo resounds: but always as "criticism", while shortly before the critic did not even dream of the possibility of the event. Nowhere does it come to have an effect but always only "criticism"; and criticism itself again has no effect but only comes to see further criticism. In view of this there has come to be general agreement that much criticism is to be seen as an effect and little or none as failure. Basically, how-

17. There is a play here on the Latin "corpora" (plural of *corpus* which can mean either a body, e.g. of a human being, or a collection of literary works). The point is that these fellows dissect the Greek poets as though they were vile and cheap bodies, while only their own literary works are vile and cheap.

18. An allusion to the last two lines of Goethe's *Faust*, part II.

ever, even with such "effect", all remains as it was: for a while one prat-
tles something new, then again something new, and in the meantime does
what one has always done. The historical education of our critics does
not permit any more that there be an effect in the proper sense, namely
an effect on life and action: on the blackest script they immediately press
their blotter, on the most graceful drawing they smear their thick brush
strokes, which are to be seen as corrections: once again it was all over.
Their critical pen, however, never ceases to flow for they have lost con-
trol over it and are directed by it, instead of directing it. Just in this
immoderation of their critical effusion, in this lack of self-mastery, in
what the Romans call *impotentia*, the weakness of the modern personality is betrayed.

6

But let us leave this weakness be. Rather let us turn to a much praised
strength of modern man with the question, which to be sure is embar-
rassing, whether he has a right by virtue of his well known historical "objectivity" to call himself strong, that is, *just,* and that to a higher degree
than the man of other times. Is it true that this objectivity has its origin in a
heightened desire and demand for justice? Or does it, as the effect of quite
different causes, merely make it seem that justice is the proper cause of this
effect? Does it perhaps mislead to a prejudice, dangerous because all too
flattering, about the virtues of modern man?—Socrates took it to be a
malady approaching insanity to imagine that one possesses a virtue when
one does not possess it: and certainly such imagination is more dangerous
than the opposite delusion of suffering from a shortcoming, from a vice.
For through this delusion it is perhaps still possible to become better; the
former imagination, however, will daily make a man or an age worse, that
is—in this case, more unjust.

Truly, no one has more of a right to our respect than he who possesses
the drive and strength to justice. For in it are joined and hidden the highest
and rarest virtues as in an unfathomable sea which receives and swallows
up rivers from all sides. The hand of the just man who is competent to sit
in judgment no longer trembles when it holds the scales; pitiless toward
himself he places weight upon weight, he is not downcast when the scales
rise or fall and his voice is neither harsh nor broken when he proclaims the
verdict. Were he a cold demon of knowledge he would spread about
himself an icy atmosphere of superhumanly terrible majesty which we
would have to fear, not revere: but that he is a man and attempts to rise
from trivial doubt to strict certainty, from tolerant mildness to the imperative 'you must', from the rare virtue of generosity to the rarest of
justice, that he now resembles that demon without from the beginning being anything other than a poor man, and above all that at every moment
he must in himself do penance for his humanity and tragically devours

himself through his impossible virtue—all this places him upon a solitary height as the most *venerable* exemplar of the species man; for he wants truth but not only as cold knowledge without consequences, rather as ordering and punishing judge, truth not as the egoistic possession of the individual but as the sacred justification to shift all boundary markers of egoistic possessions, in a word, truth as the Last Judgment and certainly not as the chance prey and pleasure of the individual hunter. Only so far as the seeker after truth has the unconditional will to be just is there something great in the striving for truth which is everywhere glorified so thoughtlessly: while before the duller eye quite a number of the most diverse drives such as curiosity, flight from boredom, envy, vanity, play instinct—drives which have nothing at all to do with truth—merge with that striving for truth which has its root in justice. The world may appear full of those who "serve truth"; and yet the virtue of justice is found so rarely, more rarely yet is it recognized and almost always mortally hated: whereas the host of sham virtues has at all times paraded in honour and pomp. Few serve truth in truth because only few have the pure will to be just, and of those again very few have the strength to be just. It is not at all sufficient to have only the will to justice: and the most terrible sufferings have come upon man precisely from a drive to justice which lacks power of judgment; which is why the general welfare would require no more than to strew the seed of the power of judgment as widely as possible so that the fanatic remain distinct from the judge, the blind desire to be a judge distinct from the conscious power of being allowed to judge. But where is there a means of planting the power of judgment!—that is why men, whenever one speaks to them of truth and justice, will forever tarry in hesitant indecision whether the fanatic or the judge speaks to them. One ought therefore forgive them if they have always greeted with particular good will those "servants of truth" who have neither the will nor the power to judge and set themselves the task of seeking "pure" knowledge "without consequences" or, more plainly, truth that comes to nothing. There are very many indifferent truths; there are problems about which to judge correctly requires not even effort, to say nothing of sacrifice. A man may well succeed in becoming a cold demon of knowledge in this indifferent harmless area; and nevertheless! Even if in particularly favoured times whole cohorts of scholars and researchers are transformed into such demons—regrettably it still remains possible that such a time suffers from deficiency in strict and great justice—in short, in the noblest core of the so-called impulse to truth.

Consider now the historical virtuoso of the present time: is he the justest man of his age? It is true, he has developed in himself such a delicate and sensitive sensibility that nothing human remains alien to him; the most diverse ages and persons immediately reverberate in familiar sounds on his lyre: he has become a reverberating passivity which with its sounds acts again on other such passivities: until finally the whole atmosphere of an age is filled with a buzzing confusion of such tender and familiar reverberations. Yet it seems to me that one perceives, as it were, only the overtones of every original historical key-note: what was robust and powerful in the original can no longer be guessed in the ethereally thin and pointed sound of those strings. Moreover, the original note usually woke deeds, needs, terror, this one lulls us to sleep and turns us into soft men of pleasure; it is as though the heroic symphony[19] had been arranged for two flutes and reserved for the use of dreamy opium smokers. From this one may already gauge how matters will stand with these virtuosos as regards the chief claim of modern man to higher and purer justice; this virtue never has anything appealing about it, knows no exciting rush of emotion, is hard and terrible. Measured by it how low in the ranks of virtues is even generosity, that quality of a few rare historians! But a great many more only get as far as tolerance, as far as letting stand what simply cannot be denied, as far as ordering and beautifying with measured benevolence, on the clever assumption that the inexperienced will interpret it as the virtue of justice when the past is recounted without any harsh accents and without the expression of hatred. But only superior power can judge and weakness must tolerate if it would not feign strength and make an actress of justice on her seat of judgment. Yet there is still left over one dreadful species of historian, of diligent, strict and honest character—but narrow-minded; here the good will to be just is present, as well as the pathos of judging: but all verdicts are false for approximately the same reason that the judgments of the usual juries are false. How unlikely, then, is the frequency of historical talent! Leaving quite out of account disguised egoists and partisans who play their evil game with quite an objective bearing. Also leaving out of account those quite unreflective people who, as historians, write in the naive belief that just their age is right in all its popular opinions and that to write in accordance with the times comes to the same thing as being just; a belief in which every religion lives and concerning which, in a religious context, nothing further is to be said. Those naive historians call measuring past opinions and deeds by the common opinions of the moment "objectivity": here they find the canon of all truths; their work is to make the past fit the triviality of their time. On the other hand they call "subjective" all historical writing which does not take those popular opinions as its canon.

And might not an illusion lurk even in the highest interpretation of the word 'objectivity'? By this word one understands a condition in the historian in which his view of an event with all of its motives and consequences is so pure that it has no effect at all on his subjectivity: one has in mind that aesthetic phenomenon, that detachment from all personal in-

19. Beethoven's third symphony, the *Eroica*, is meant.

terest with which the painter sees his inner picture in a stormy landscape amid lightning and thunder or on a rough sea, one has in mind the total absorption in things: yet it is a superstition to believe that the picture which things produce in a man in such a state of mind reproduces the empirical essence of those things. Or is one to think that things in such moments, as it were, retrace, counterfeit, reproduce themselves photographically on a pure passivity through their own activity?

That would be a mythology and a bad one to boot: besides one forgets that that moment is just the most powerful and spontaneous moment of creation in the inner being of the artist, a moment of composition of the highest possible kind whose result may well be an artistically true portrait but not an historically true one. To think history objectively in this manner is the silent work of the dramatist; that is, to think everything in conjunction, to weave a whole out of the isolated: everywhere with the presupposition that a unity of plan must be put into things if it is not there. So man spins his web over the past and subdues it, so his impulse to art expresses itself—but not his impulse to truth and justice. Objectivity and justice have nothing to do with each other. One could think of a kind of historical writing which would not contain a drop of common empirical truth and yet be entitled in the highest degree to the predicate 'objectivity'. Grillparzer goes so far as to say: "what else is history, after all, than the way in which the spirit of man apprehends what for him are *impenetrable events;* unites elements of which God only knows whether they belong together; replaces the unintelligible with something intelligible; introduces its concepts of externally oriented purpose into a whole which surely admits only purposes with an inner orientation; and again assumes chance where a thousand little causes were at work. Every person at the same time has his individual necessity so that millions run in directions parallel to each other in crooked and straight lines, cross, support and restrict each other, strive forward and backward and in this assume the character of chance for each other, and so, leaving out of account the influences of natural events, make it impossible to demonstrate a penetrating all-inclusive necessity of events." Just such a necessity, however, is to be brought to light as a result of that "objective" view of things! This is a presupposition which, when stated as a dogma by the historian, can take only a curious form; Schiller, of course, is quite clear about what is properly subjective in this assumption when he says of the historian: "one appearance after the other begins to withdraw from blind approximation, from lawless freedom, and as a fit member joins the ranks of a coherent whole—*which, of course, only exists in his imagination.*"[20] But what is one to think of the claim of a famous historical virtuoso, a claim presented

20. In 1789 Friedrich Schiller became a professor of history at the University of Jena. The quotation is from his inaugural lecture delivered on May 26 and 27, 1789. The emphasized phrase is in parentheses in Schiller.

with innocent faith, artfully hovering between tautology and absurdity: "it is not otherwise than that all human acts and endeavours are subject to the silent, often imperceptible, yet powerful and inexorable course of things?" In such a proposition one discerns no more enigmatical wisdom than unenigmatical folly; as in the saying of Goethe's court gardener: "nature may let herself be forced but not compelled", or in the notice on a booth at the fair of which Swift tells: "here is to be seen the largest elephant in the world with the exception of itself". For, after all, what is the opposition between the acts and endeavours of man and the course of things? In general I notice that such historians, as the one whom we have just quoted, cease to be instructive as soon as they generalize and in doing so show the feeling of their weakness in obscurities. In other sciences the generalities are what is most important so far as they contain laws: should propositions like the one quoted pretend to be laws however, then one could reply that the historian's labour in writing history is wasted; for what remains at all true in such propositions, after deduction of that dark and insoluble remainder of which we have spoken—is well known and even trivial; for the smallest range of experience brings it to the attention of everyone. But to trouble whole peoples for this and to expend years of difficult labour to this end is surely no different from heaping experiment upon experiment in the natural sciences long after the law can already be inferred from the available store of experiments: from which senseless excess of experimentation, incidentally, contemporary natural science suffers according to Zöllner.[21] If the value of a drama lies merely in its final and main thought, then the drama itself would be a very long, crooked and laborious way to its goal; and so I hope that history may not see its significance in general thoughts as a kind of bloom and fruit: rather that its value is just this, to describe with insight a known, perhaps common theme, an everyday melody, to elevate it, raise to a comprehensive symbol and so let a whole world of depth of meaning, power and beauty be guessed in it.

But this requires above all a great artistic capacity, and creative overview, a loving immersion in the empirical data, a poetic elaboration of given types—this, to be sure, requires objectivity, but as a positive property. Objectivity, however, is so often only a phrase. The dark tranquility of the artist's eye, flashing within yet unmoved without, is replaced by the affectation of tranquility; as lack of pathos and moral strength usually disguises itself as penetrating coolness of observation. In certain cases banality of sentiment and everyday wisdom, which by being so boring give the impression of tranquility and calm, dare to step forth and pretend to be that artistic condition in which the subject is silent and becomes quite imperceptible. Then all those items which do not arouse at all are searched

21. The astrophysicist Johann Karl Friedrich Zöllner (1836-1882).

out and the dullest word is just right. One goes so far as to assume that whoever is *quite unconcerned* about a past event has a calling to describe it. Philologists and Greeks relate to each other in this way: they are of no concern to each other—and this one is pleased to call "objectivity"! Where just the highest and rarest is to be described, there intentional and openly displayed detachment, the fabricated and soberly flat motivational artifice, is nothing short of outrageous—when, that is, the *vanity* of the historian impels to this indifference parading as objectivity. Moreover one's judgment on such authors should to a considerable degree be motivated by the principle that a man has just as much vanity as he lacks understanding. No, at least be honest! Do not seek the semblance of that artistic power which is true objectivity, do not seek the semblance of justice if you are not ordained to the terrible calling of the just man. As though, moreover, it were the task of every age that it must be just about everything past! As a matter of fact ages and generations never have the right to be the judge of all earlier ages and generations: rather such an uncomfortable mission occasionally is the lot only of individuals, and the rarest at that. Who forces you to judge? And then—just inquire of yourselves whether you could be just even if you wanted to! As judges you must stand higher than the one to be judged; while you have only come later. The guests who are the last to arrive at table justifiably should receive the last places: and you want to have the first? Well then, at least do the highest and greatest; perhaps one will really make room for you then, even if you arrive last.

Only from the standpoint of the highest strength of the present may you interpret the past: only in the highest exertion of your noblest qualities will you discern what is worthy of being known and preserved, what is great in the past. Like by like! Otherwise you will draw the past down to yourselves. Do not believe any historical writing if it does not issue from the head of the rarest minds; but you will always notice the quality of mind of such writing when it is required to assert something general or to repeat something generally known: the genuine historian must have the strength to recast the well known into something never heard before and to proclaim the general so simply and profoundly that one overlooks its simplicity because of its profundity and its profundity because of its simplicity. No one can be a great historian, an artistic man and a shallowpate at the same time: however one should not despise the workers who cart, heap up and sift because it is certain that they cannot become great historians; and even less should one confuse them with those historians but rather understand them to be the necessary helpers and underlings in the service of the master: somewhat as the French, with greater naïveté than is possible among the Germans, used to speak of the *historiens de M. Thiers.*[22] These workers should gradually become great scholars, but can never be masters for all that. A great scholar and a great shallowpate—that will more easily go together under one hat.

So: history is written by the experienced and superior man. If you have not had some higher and greater experiences than all others you will not know how to interpret anything great and high in the past. The past always speaks as an oracle: only as master builders of the future who know the present will you understand it. We now explain the extraordinarily deep and extensive effect of Delphi especially by the fact that the priests of Delphi had exact knowledge of the past; now it is proper to know that only the builder of the future has a right to judge the past. By looking forward and setting a great goal for yourselves you will also curb that rank impulse to analysis which now lays waste your present and almost makes impossible all calm and all peaceful growth and ripening. Draw about yourselves the fence of a great and embracing hope, a hopeful striving. Form an image for yourselves to which the future ought to correspond and forget the superstitition that you are epigoni. You have enough to ponder and invent by pondering that future life; but do not ask history to show the How? and Wherewith?. If, on the other hand, you live yourselves into the history of great men you will learn from it a highest commandment, to become ripe and to flee from that paralyzing educational constraint of the age, which sees its advantage in preventing your becoming ripe, in order to rule and to exploit you unripe ones. And if you want biographies then not those with the refrain "Mr. So-and-so and His Time" but rather those on whose title page should be inscribed "A Fighter Against His Time". Satisfy your souls on Plutarch and dare to believe in yourselves when you believe in his heroes. A hundred such men educated against the modern fashion, that is, men who have ripened and are used to the heroic, could now silence forever the whole noisy pseudo-education of our time.

7

The historical sense, if it rules *without restraint* and unfolds all its implications, uproots the future because it destroys illusions and robs existing things of their atmosphere in which alone they can live. Historical justice, even when it is practised truly and with pure intentions, is a terrible virtue because it always undermines the living and brings it to ruin: its judging is always annihilating. If no constructive drive is active behind the historical drive, if one does not destroy and clear away so that a future, already alive in our hope, may build its house on the cleared ground, if

22. Louis Adolphe Thiers (1797-1877), French politician, journalist and historian, whose *Histoire du consulat et de l'empire* was published in twenty volumes between 1845 and 1862.

justice alone rules, then the creative instinct is enfeebled and discouraged. A religion for example which, under the rule of pure justice, is to be transformed into historical knowledge, a religion which is to be thoroughly known in a scientific way, will at the end of this path also be annihilated. The reason is that the historical audit always brings to light so much that is false, crude, inhuman, absurd, violent, that the attitude of pious illusion, in which alone all that wants to live can live, is necessarily dispelled: only with love, however, only surrounded by the shadow of the illusion of love, can man create, that is, only with an unconditional faith in something perfect and righteous. Each man who is forced no longer to love unconditionally has had the root of his strength cut off: he must wither, that is, become dishonest. In such effects art is opposed to history: and only if history can bear being transformed into a work of art, that is, to become a pure art form, may it perhaps preserve instincts or even rouse them. But such a manner of writing history would thoroughly contradict the analytic and inartistic trend of our time, it would even be perceived as falsification. But history which only destroys without being guided by an inner constructive drive will in the long run make its instruments blasé and unnatural: for such men destroy illusions and "whoever destroys illusion in himself and others will be punished by nature, the strictest tyrant."[23] For some considerable time one may well occupy oneself with history quite harmlessly and unreflectively as though it were an occupation as good as any other; especially recent theology appears quite innocently to have taken up history and even now is hardly aware that in doing so, probably quite against its will, it has entered the service of Voltaire's écrasez.[24] Let no one suppose new and powerful constructive instincts behind this; one would then have to let the so-called Protestant Union count as the cradle of a new religion and the jurist Holtzendorf (the man who edited and wrote the preface to what is still widely called the Protestant Bible) might have to be acknowledged as John by the river Jordan. For a time perhaps the Hegelian philosophy, still smoking in older heads, may help to propagate that innocence, say, in that one distinguishes the "Idea of Christianity" from its many inadequate "forms of appearing" and talks oneself into thinking that it is the "love play of the Idea" to reveal itself in ever purer forms until finally it achieves the certainly purest, most transparent, hardly visible form in the brain of the contemporary

---

23. Cf. J. W. von Goethe, Schriften zur Natur- und Wissenschaftslehre, Fragment über die Natur, in Artemis - Gedenkausgabe der Werke, Briefe und Gespräche, ed. Ernst Beutler, Zürich und Stuttgart, 1948 ff., Vol. 16, p. 923. The quotation also occurs in E. von Hartmann, Philosophie des Unbewußten, Berlin, 1869, p. 620. Nietzsche probably drew his quotation from here since it exactly matches von Hartmann's slight changes in Goethe's text.

24. Ecrasez l'infâme: (literally) crush the infamous one. Voltaire's motto aimed at superstition and fanaticism impeding the progress of rational thought, thus, indirectly, at the Christian church.

theologus liberalis vulgaris.[25] But if you listen to these most purified forms of Christianity talk about the earlier less purified forms then the impartial listener often gets the impression that it is not at all Christianity which is being discussed but rather—well, what are we to think of when we find Christianity characterized by "the greatest theologian of the century" as the religion which allows one "to feel oneself into all actual and a few merely possible religions", and when the "true church" is said to be the one which "becomes a fluid mass which knows no outline, in which each part is found at times here at times there and everything mingles peacefully"? Again, what are we to think of?

What one can learn from Christianity, that as a result of a historicizing treatment it has become blasé and unnatural until finally a completely historical, that is, just treatment has resolved it into pure knowledge about Christianity and so has annihilated it, all this one can study in everything that has life: that it ceases to live when it has been dissected completely and lives painfully and becomes sick once one begins to practise historical dissection on it. There are men who believe in the overturning, reforming, healing powers of German music among Germans: they are angered and deem it an injustice, perpetrated on what is most alive in our culture, when men such as Mozart and Beethoven already get buried under the whole learned rubbish of biography and are forced to answer a thousand impertinent questions by the systematic torture of historical criticism. Is not something, which in its living effect is not at all exhausted, done away with too soon, or at least paralyzed, when greedy curiosity is directed on countless minutiae of life and works and when one searches for intellectual problems where one ought to learn to live and forget all problems? Just imagine a few such modern biographers transferred to the birthplace of Christianity or the Lutheran Reformation; their sober pragmatizing curiosity might just have sufficed to make impossible every ghostly *actio in distans:*[26] or the most miserable animal can prevent the genesis of the mightiest oak by swallowing the acorn. Every living thing needs to be surrounded by an atmosphere, a mysterious circle of mist: if one robs it of this veil, if one condemns a religion, an art, a genius to orbit as a star without an atmosphere: then one should not wonder about its rapidly becoming withered, hard and barren. That is just how it is with all things great indeed,

"which without some madness ne'er succeed"[27]

as Hans Sachs says in *Die Meistersinger*.

25. The common liberal theologian.

26. Action at a distance.

27. Hans Sachs sings this line in Act III of Wagner's opera *Die Meistersinger von Nürnberg*.

But every people, even every man, who wants to become *ripe* needs such an enveloping madness, such a protective and veiling cloud; now, however, we hate ripening as such because history is honoured above life. One even sees cause to triumph in the fact that "science now begins to rule life": perhaps this will be achieved; but surely a life ruled in that way is not worth much because it is much less *life* and guarantees much less life for the future than the life which used to be ruled not by knowledge but by instincts and powerful illusion. But then, as I have said, it is not to be an age of finished, ripe and harmonious personalities but of common, maximally useful labour. Yet that merely signified: men are to be trained for the purposes of the age to lend a hand as soon as possible: they are to labour in the factory of common utility before they are ripe, or rather to prevent their ever becoming ripe—because that would be a luxury which would withdraw a lot of strength from "the labour market". One blinds some birds to make them sing more beautifully: I do not believe that today's men sing more beautifully than their grandfathers, but I do know that they are blinded early. But the means, the vile means used to blind them is *much too bright, much too sudden, much too changeable light.* The young man is whipped through all millennia: youths who understand nothing of war, of diplomatic action, of commercial policy are deemed worthy of being introduced to political history. But just as the young man runs through history so we moderns run through art galleries, so we listen to concerts. One may well feel that this sounds different from that, this makes a different impression from that: increasingly to lose this sense of surprise, no longer to be excessively astonished by anything, finally to tolerate everything—that is what we call historical sense, historical culture. To say it without making excuses: the flood of influences is so massive, the surprising, barbaric, violent crowds so overwhelmingly, "rolled into ugly clumps", upon the youthful soul, that it can only save itself by deliberately dulling its sensibility. With a finer and stronger consciousness we may well find another sentiment: disgust. The young man has become so homeless and doubts all customs and concepts. Now he knows it: things were different in all ages, it does not matter how you are. In melancholy apathy he lets opinion upon opinion pass by him and understands the meaning of Hölderlin's words and mood when reading Diogenes Laertius concerning the lives and teachings of Greek philosophers: "here too I have experienced again what I have already noted a number of times, namely that the ephemeral and changing in human thoughts and systems has impressed me as being almost more tragic than the fates which alone one usually calls the actual ones."[28] No, such flooding, numbing, violent historicizing is certainly not required for

---

28. Friedrich Hölderlin's letter to Isaak von Sinclair dated December 24, 1798.

youth as the ancients show, rather it is dangerous in the highest degree as
the moderns show. Now, however, consider the historical student, the
heir of a blasé indifference which appears all too soon, almost in his
boyhood. Now he has acquired the "method" for his own work, the correct technique and the refined tone in the manner of his master; a quite
isolated little chapter of the past has fallen victim to his acuteness and the
method he has learned; he has already produced or, to use a prouder
word, he has "created", he has now become a servant of truth in deed and
lord of the world of history. If he was "done" already as a boy, then he is
now overdone: you only need to shake him and wisdom will fall into your
lap with great rattling; yet the wisdom is rotten and every apple has its
worm. Believe me: if men are to labour and become useful in the scientific
factory before they are ripe, science will soon be ruined as well as the
slaves put to use all too soon in this factory. I regret that one is already required to use the linguistic jargon of slaveholders and employers in order
to describe such conditions which ought to be thought basically free of
utilities and exempted from the struggle for survival; but the words 'factory', 'labour market', 'offer', 'utilization'—and all the rest of the auxiliary
verbs[29] of egoism—involuntarily throng to one's lips if one wants to
describe the youngest generation of scholars. Sterling mediocrity becomes
ever more mediocre and science ever more useful in the economic sense.
Actually the newest scholars are wise in only one respect and in this admittedly wiser than all men of the past, in all other respects only infinitely different—to put it carefully—from all scholars of the old type. Nevertheless
they demand honours and advantages for themselves, as though the state
and public opinion were obligated to take the new coin just as seriously as
the old. The carters have entered into a labour contract with each other
and decreed the genius to be superfluous—for every carter is being
stamped a genius; probably a later age will be able to tell that their struc-
tures have been carted together, not joined together. Those who tirelessly
use the modern cry of battle and sacrifice "Division of labour! Fall into
line!" are for once to be told clearly and bluntly: if you want to further
science as quickly as possible you will destroy it as quickly as possible; as
the hen will perish if artificially forced to lay eggs too quickly. Granted,
science has been furthered surprisingly quickly in the last decades: but just
look at the scholars, the exhausted hens. They truly are no "harmonious"
natures; they can only cackle more than ever because they lay eggs more
often: of course, the eggs have become ever smaller (even if the books ever
bigger). As the last and natural result we find the universally favoured
"popularization" (next to "feminization" and "infantization") of science,
that is the infamous re-cutting of the garment of science to fit a "mixed
public"; to use tailor's German to describe a tailor's activity. Goethe saw a

---

29. This seems odd after that list of nouns. But the same oddity is found in the German.

misuse in this and demanded that the sciences have an effect on the external world only through an *elevated practice*. Older generations of scholars
moreover deemed such a misuse difficult and burdensome for good
reason: equally for good reason it is easy for the younger scholars because
they themselves, apart from a very small corner of knowledge, are a very
mixed public and have its needs. They only need on occasion to sit down
comfortably and they succeed in opening up their own little area of study
as well to that mixed popular need and curiosity. Such a comfortable act
one later calls pretentiously "modest condescension of a scholar to his people": while at bottom the scholar only descended to himself so far as he is
not a scholar but a plebeian. Create for yourselves the concept of a "people": that concept you can never think nobly nor highly enough. Were you
to think highly of the people you would also be merciful to them and
would beware of offering them your historical *aqua fortis*[30] as a quickening refreshing drink. But at bottom, you think very little of them because
you are not permitted a true and well founded respect for their future, and
you act as practical pessimists, I mean as men who are guided by a
premonition of ruin and therefore become indifferent and careless of the
welfare of others and even of their own. As long as the earth will still bear
us! And if it will no longer bear us we can accept that too:—thus they feel
and live an *ironical* existence.

8

It may appear surprising but should not be thought contradictory if
despite the age's noisy, obtrusive and carefree rejoicing about its historical
culture I nevertheless ascribe a kind of *ironical self-consciousness* to it, a
pervasive inkling that there is no cause for rejoicing, a fear that perhaps all
enjoyment of historical knowledge will soon be gone. A similar puzzle
concerning individual personalities has been offered us by Goethe in his
remarkable characterization of Newton: he finds in the depths (or more
correctly: at the heights) of his being "an obscure inkling of his error", as
though there were an expression, perceptible at particular moments, of a
superior judging consciousness which has achieved a certain ironical overview of its necessary inner nature. So one finds especially in the greater
and more highly developed historical men a consciousness, often subdued
to the point of general scepticism, of how great is the absurdity and
superstition in the belief that the education of a people must be as
predominantly historical as it is now; after all, the strongest peoples,
strong, that is, in deeds and works, have lived differently, have raised
their youth differently. But that absurdity, that superstition suits us—so
goes the sceptical objection—us the latecomers, us the faded last shoots of

---

30. Nitric acid. Literally, strong water.

mighty and cheerful generations, us to whom Hesiod's prophecy applies that men would one day be born with grey hair and that Zeus would destroy this generation as soon as that sign has become visible in it. Historical education really is a kind of inborn grayheadedness, and those who bear its mark from childhood on surely must attain the instinctive belief in the *old age of mankind:* it is now fitting for old age, however, to engage in the activity of old men, that is, to look back, to tally and close our accounts, to seek consolation in the past through memories, in short, historical education. But the race of man is a tough and enduring thing and does not, after millennia, hardly even after hundreds of thousands of years, want to be observed in its steps—forward and backward—that is, it does *not at all* want to be observed as a whole by that infinitesimally small atomic speck, the individual man. Of what account, after all, are a couple of millennia (or expressed differently: the period of 34 consecutive lives of men calculated at 60 years each) that at the beginning of such a time we can still speak of a "youth" and at the end of it already of an "old age of mankind"! Does not this paralyzing belief in an already withering mankind rather harbour the misunderstanding, inherited from the Middle Ages, of a Christian theological conception, the thought that the end of the world is near, of the fearfully expected judgment? Does that conception appear in different guise through the heightened historical need to judge, as though our age, the last possible one, were itself qualified to conduct the last judgment of the whole past which the Christian faith expected not at all from man but from "the Son of Man"? At an earlier time this *"memento mori"*[31] addressed to mankind as well as the individual, was always a torturing thorn and, as it were, the high point of medieval knowledge and conscience. The counter dictum of a more recent time: *"memento vivere"*[32] frankly still sounds quite timid, lacks full-throated power and almost has something dishonest about it. For mankind is still tied to the *memento mori* and betrays it in its universal historical need: despite the most powerful beat of its wings knowledge has been unable to tear itself loose and attain freedom, a deep feeling of hopelessness has remained and has taken on that historical colouration by which all higher education and culture is now surrounded in melancholy darkness. A religion which, of all the hours of a human life, takes the last one to be the most important, which predicts an end to life on earth as such and condemns the living to live in the fifth act of the tragedy surely stimulates the deepest and noblest powers, but is hostile toward all new planting, bold attempting, free desiring; it resists every flight into the unknown because it does not love there, does not hope there: it lets all becoming be forced on it only against its will in order, in good time, to push it aside or sacrifice it as

31. Remember you must die.

32. Remember to live.

a temptation to existence, as a liar about the value of existence. What the Florentines did when, under the influence of Savonarola's penitential sermons, they committed paintings, manuscripts, mirrors and masks to those famed sacrificial flames, Christianity would like to do to every culture which incites to striving further and takes for its motto *memento vivere;* and if it is not possible to do this straightforwardly and without detour, that is through superior strength, it nevertheless attains its end if it allies itself with historical education, in most cases even without the latter's complicity, and now, speaking through this education, rejects with a shrug of the shoulders everything in the process of becoming and spreads over it the feeling of being very late arrivals and epigoni, in short, of being congenitally grey haired. The austere, deeply serious observation concerning the valuelessness of all that has been, concerning the ripeness of the world for judgment has dispersed itself into the sceptical consciousness that at any rate it is good to know all that has been since it is too late to do something better. In this way the historical sense makes its servants passive and retrospective; and almost only from momentary forgetfulness, at a brief period of inactivity of that sense, does the man struck ill by historical fever become active, only to dissect his deed as soon as it is done and by observing it analytically to prevent its having any further effect and finally to pare it down to "history". In this sense we still live in the Middle Ages and history is still a disguised theology: just as the reverence which the layman accords the scientific caste is a reverence inherited from the clergy. What earlier one gave to the church one now gives, even if more sparingly, to science: but that one gives at all is a consequence of the church and not of the modern spirit which rather, along with its other good qualities, is known to be somewhat miserly and a bungler when it comes to the noble virtue of liberality.

Perhaps this observation does not please, perhaps just as little as the above derivation of the excess of history from the medieval *memento mori* and from the hopelessness which Christianity bears in its heart toward all coming times of earthly existence. But then let this explanation, which I offer with some doubt to be sure, be replaced by better explanations; for the origin of historical education—and its inner quite radical contradiction with the spirit of a "new age", a "modern consciousness"—this origin *must* itself in turn be historically understood, history *must* itself dissolve the problem of history, knowledge *must* turn its sting against itself—this threefold *must* is the imperative of the spirit of the "new age" if it really does contain something new, mighty, original and a promise of life. Or should it be true that we Germans—to leave the Romance peoples out of account—must in all higher matters of culture always only be "descendants" because this is all we *could* be; as Wilhelm Wackernagel[33] once

33. Carl Heinrich Wilhelm Wackernagel (1806 1869) was, next to Jacob Grimm, the most eminent Germanist of his time. I have been unable to find the reference in either of two works by Wackernagel which Nietzsche owned.

asserted this proposition, one well worth pondering: "We Germans simply are a people of descendants, we are with all our higher knowledge and even with our faith always only successors of the ancient world; even the hostile ones who do not want it constantly breathe, beside the spirit of Christianity, the immortal spirit of ancient classical culture, and were one to succeed in eliminating these two elements from the vital air surrounding the inner man then not much would remain to sustain a spiritual life." But even if we could content ourselves with the vocation of being descendants of antiquity, even were we to resolve emphatically to take it seriously and conceive it greatly and in this emphasis to recognize our distinguishing and sole prerogative—we would nevertheless be constrained to ask whether it must eternally be our destiny *to be pupils of fading antiquity:* at some time it may be allowed step by step to set our goal higher and farther, at some time we ought to be allowed to claim the merit of having recreated in ourselves—also through our universal history—the spirit of Alexandrian-Roman culture so fruitfully and magnificently as now to be entitled, as the noblest reward, to set ourselves the still mightier task of striving behind and beyond this Alexandrian world and courageously to seek our standards of the great, the natural and human in the ancient Greek world. *But there we will also find the actuality of an essentially unhistorical culture and a culture which is nevertheless, or rather therefore, unspeakably rich and full of life.* Even were we Germans nothing but descendants—we could, by looking upon such a culture as an inheritance to be appropriated, be nothing greater and prouder than just descendants.

Only this and nothing but this is meant here, that even the frequently distressing thought of being epigoni, when grandly conceived, may vouchsafe great effects and a hopeful desire for the future, in the individual as well as in a people: in so far, that is, as we conceive ourselves to be the heirs and successors of classical and astonishing powers, and see in that our honour and incentive. Not then as pale and feeble late arrivals of vigorous generations who eke out a frosty life as antiquarians and grave diggers of those generations. Such late arrivals, of course, live an ironic existence: annihilation follows upon the heels of their limping course through life; they shudder at the thought of this annihilation as they enjoy the past, for they are living memories, but, without heirs, their memory is meaningless. So the dull inkling overcomes them that their life is an injustice, for no coming life can justify it.

Yet were we to think of such antiquarian late arrivals as suddenly exchanging that ironically painful modesty for shamelessness; let us think of them as with shrill voices they proclaim: the race is at its height, for only now does it know itself and has become revealed to itself—we would then have a spectacle in which, as in a parable, we could discover the significance of a certain very famous philosophy for German education. I believe that there has been no dangerous change or turn in the German education of this century which has not become more dangerous through the enormous influence, continuing to the present moment, of this philosophy, the Hegelian. Truly the belief that one is a late arrival of the ages is paralyzing and upsetting: terrible and destructive it must seem, however, if one day such a belief, by a bold inversion, deifies this late arrival as the true meaning and purpose of all that has happened earlier, if his knowing misery is equated with a consummation of world history. Such a way of looking at things has accustomed the Germans to talk of the "world-process" and to justify their own time as the necessary result of this world-process; such a way of looking at things has established history in place of the other spiritual powers, art and religion, as solely sovereign in so far as it is "the self-realizing concept", in so far as it is "the dialectic of the spirit of people" and the "Last Judgment".

This history, understood in a Hegelian way, has contemptuously been called the sojourn of God on earth, which God, however, is himself first produced by history. But this God became transparent and intelligible to himself inside the Hegelian craniums and has already ascended all possible dialectical steps of his becoming up to that self-revelation: so that for Hegel the apex and terminus of world history coincided in his own Berlin existence. He should even have said that all things after him are properly judged to be only a musical coda of the world-historical rondo; more properly yet, to be redundant. He did not say that: and so he implanted in the generation thoroughly leavened by him that admiration for the "power of history" which practically at every moment turns into naked admiration for success and leads to the idolatry of the factual: for which service one has now generally memorized the very mythological, but apart from that quite good German turn of phrase 'to take the facts into account'. But who once has learned to bend his back and bow his head before the "power of history" finally nods his "yes", mechanically like a Chinese, to every power, be this a government or a public opinion or a numerical majority, and moves his limbs precisely in the tempo in which some "power" or other pulls the string. If every success contains within itself a rational necessity, if every event is a victory of the logical or of the "idea"—then quickly down on your knees and up and down on every rung of the step ladder of "success"! What, there are no more ruling mythologies? What, religions are about to become extinct? Just look at the religion of historical power, take note of the priests of the idea-mythology and their abused knees! Are not even all the virtues adherents of this new faith? Or is it not selflessness when historical man permits himself to be drained to the point of becoming an objective looking glass? Is it not generosity to renounce all authority in heaven and on earth by worshiping authority as such in every authority? Is it not justice always to have the scales of powers ready to hand and always to observe meticulously which, as the stronger and heavier, will tip the balance? And what a school of decorum it is to contemplate history in this way! To take everything objectively, not to be angered by anything, to love nothing, to comprehend everything, how gentle and pliable this makes one; and even if someone raised in this school on occasion is publicly angry and frets, one is pleased by this for one knows that it is only meant artistically, it is *ira* and *studium*, and yet through and through *sine ira et studio*.[34]

What antiquated thoughts I harbour in my breast toward such a complex of mythology and virtue! But they must out for once, and may everyone have a good laugh. I would say the following: history always inculcates: "once upon a time", the moral: "you ought not" or "you ought not to have". So history becomes a compendium of actual immorality. How grievously he would err who would at the same time view history as the judge of this actual immorality! That a Raphael had to die at the age of thirty-six, for example, is offensive to morality: such a being ought never to die. If now you want to come to the aid of history, as apologists of the actual, you will say: he expressed all he had to say and given a longer life he would always only have produced beauty as the same beauty, not as new beauty, and things of this sort. Thus you are advocates of the devil, namely by making of success, of fact, your idol: while a fact is always stupid and has at all times resembled a calf more than a god. As apologists of history, moreover, you are prompted to ignorance: for only because you do not know what such a *natura naturans*[35] as Raphael is do you not begin to seethe when you realized that he existed and will exist no more. Someone has recently wanted to instruct us that at the age of 82 Goethe was burned out: and yet I would gladly exchange a few years of the "burned out" Goethe for whole cart loads of fresh ultra-modern lives, so as still to have a share of such conversations as Goethe held with Eckermann,[36] and so as to be preserved from the up to date instruction of the legionaries of the moment. How few living men have any right to live, compared to such dead ones! That the many live and those few live no more is nothing but a brutal truth, that is, an incorrigible stupidity, a blunt "so it happens to be" over against the moral "it ought not to be so". Yes, over against morality! For you may talk of whatever virtue you want, of justice, generosity, courage, of the wisdom and compassion of

---

34. This presents some difficulty for the translator. Nietzsche's point is that such a man's *ira* (indignation) and *studium* (involvement) are an act, performed merely for effect, remaining a case not of *studium* (Latin: involvement) but of *Studium* (German: course of objective studies maintaining proper distance from the subject matter), i.e. it remains a case of *sine ira et studio* (without indignation and involvement), which is the phrase used by Tacitus (Annals, Ch. I) to describe his approach to Roman history.

35. Creative nature as distinct from *natura naturata* or created nature.

36. Cf. J. W. von Goethe, *Conversations with Eckermann*, M. Walter Dunne, New York and London, 1901.

man—everywhere he is virtuous only because he was outraged by that blind power of facts, by the tyranny of the actual, and subjects himself to laws which are not laws of those fluctuations of history. He always swims against the historical waves, whether he controls his passion as the nearest stupid fact of his existence or whether he commits himself to honesty while all around him lies spin their glittering nets. Were history nothing more than "the world system of passion and error" man would have to read in it as Goethe counselled that Werther[37] be read: just as though it called "be a man and do not follow me!" Fortunately, however, it also preserves the memory of the great fighters *against history*, that is, against the blind power of the actual, and puts itself in the pillory precisely by singling out just those as the proper historical natures who concerned themselves little with the "so it is" but rather followed a "so it ought to be" with merry pride. Not to carry their generation to the grave but to found a new generation—that drives them forward incessantly: and even if they are born as latecomers—there is a way of living which will erase this from memory—the coming generations will only know them as firstcomers.

9

Is our time perhaps such a firstcomer? —Indeed the vehemence of its historical sense is so great and expresses itself in such a universal and necessarily unbounded manner that coming times will praise it as a firstcomer in at least this—if, that is, there will be *coming times* at all understood in the cultural sense. But precisely this raises grave doubts. Hard by the pride of modern man we find his *irony* about himself, his awareness that he must live in a historicizing and, as it were, evening mood, his fear of being unable to save for the future any of his youthful hopes and youthful strength. Here and there one goes further, into *cynicism,* and justifies the course of history, of the total development of the world, essentially for the everyday use of modern man according to the cynical canon: exactly this moment had to come just as it is, man had to become what men are now and nothing else, no one may oppose this "must". He who cannot endure irony flees into the comfort of cynicism of this kind; the last decade, moreover, offers to make him a present of one of its most beautiful inventions, a well rounded and full phrase for that cynicism: it calls his way of living in step with the times and quite unreflectively "the total surrender of his personality to the world process". The personality and the world process! The world process and the personality of the flea-beetle! If only one did not eternally have to hear the hyperbole of all hyperboles, the word: world, world, world, since, after all, if we remain honest, everyone ought only to speak of man, man, man! Heirs of the Greeks and the Romans? of Christianity? All that seems nothing to those cynics; but

37. Goethe's novel *The Sorrows of Young Werther* is meant.

heirs of the world process! Peaks and targets of the world process! Meaning and solution to all riddles of becoming expressed in modern man, the ripest fruit on the tree of knowledge—that I call rising exultation; by this token the firstlings of all ages may be known even if they have come last. This far the contemplation of history has never yet flown, not even in a dream; for now the history of man is only the continuation of the history of animals and plants; even in the lowest depths of the sea the historical universalist still finds traces of himself, as living slime; astonished, as though it were a miracle, by the enormous road man has already come, his gaze is dizzied by the yet more astonishing miracle, by modern man himself who has attained an overview of this road. High and proud he stands on the pyramid of the world process; by placing the keystone of his knowledge on top he seems to be calling to nature listening round about: "we are at the goal, we are the goal, we are the completion of nature".

Overproud European of the nineteenth century, you are mad! Your knowledge does not complete nature but only kills your own. Just measure your height as a knower by your depth as a doer. Admittedly you climb the sunbeams of your knowledge upwards to heaven, but also downwards to chaos. Your manner of moving, that is, of climbing as a knower, is your doom; foundation and solid earth retreat into uncertainty for you; there are no more supports for your life, only gossamer threads which every new grip of your knowledge tears apart. —But not another serious word about this, since it is possible to say a cheerful one.

This madly thoughtless fragmentation and fraying of all foundations, their dissolution into an ever flowing and dispersing becoming, the tireless entangling and historicizing of all that has come to be by modern man, that great garden spider in the node of the world web—all this may occupy and worry the moralist, the artist, the pious man and perhaps the statesman as well; we, however, will for once be cheered up by it today by seeing all this in the glittering magic mirror of a *philosophical parodist* in whose head the age has achieved an ironical consciousness of itself, and that clearly "to the point of infamy" (to speak the language of Goethe). Hegel once taught us "when the spirit makes a move we philosophers are also at hand":[38] our time made a move, into self-irony, and behold!, E.

38. The spirit at issue here is the universal knowing spirit which, according to Hegel, is the proper subject of world history. The self-transforming development of this spirit, for which peoples and nations are the means, constitutes world history. The move referred to in the quotation is the transition from one form of the spirit to another. At such a time, when a form of life has fully unfolded itself and enters a decline, philosophers are at hand to perform a fourfold function. They capture the spirit of the declining age in thought; they contribute to the demise of the present form of life by attacking the morality, religion and political institutions of their day; they flee from reality into an ideal world of thought which serves as a consolation in times of decay and unhappiness; their philosophy provides a birthplace for the next form of the spirit, preparing in thought for the next world historical reality. Cf. G. W. F. Hegel, *Einleitung in die Geschichte der Philosophie*, ed. Johannes Hoffmeister (1940) and Friedhelm Nicolin (1959), Verlag von Felix Meiner, Hamburg, 1966, esp. pp. 149–155 and pp. 285–287. I have been unable to find the reference.

von Hartmann was also at hand and had written his famous philosophy of the unconscious[39] —or, to speak more clearly, his philosophy of unconscious irony. Rarely have we read a merrier invention and a more philosophical prank than Hartmann's; whoever is not enlightened about *becoming* and, more than that, does not have his inner life set in order by him, is surely a living anachronism. Beginning and end of the world process, from the first startled awakening to consciousness to its being flung back into the void, together with the precisely determined task of our generation for the world process, all this presented as flowing from the so wittily invented inspirational font of the unconscious and glowing in an apocalyptic light, everything fashioned so deceptively and with such staunch seriousness as though it really were serious philosophy and not merely a philosophical jest—such a composition establishes its creator as one of the foremost philosophical parodists of all time: let us then sacrifice on his altar, let us sacrifice a lock of hair to the inventor of a true panacea—to steal an expression of admiration from Schleiermacher.[40] For what medicine is more effective against an excess of historical education than Hartmann's parody of all world history?

Were one to say quite matter-of-factly what Hartmann proclaims to us from the smoke enshrouded tripod of unconscious irony one would say: he proclaims to us that our age need only be just as it is if humanity is for once to become thoroughly fed up with this life: which we believe with all our heart. That frightening ossification of the age, that restless rattling of bones—as David Strauß has naively depicted it for us as the most beautiful actuality—is justified by Hartmann not only from behind, *ex causis efficientibus*,[41] but even from before *ex causa finali*;[42] the rogue lets light stream over our age from judgment day and so it is found to be very good, for him, that is, who wants to suffer as much as possible from the indigestibility of life and for whom that judgment day cannot arrive soon enough. To be sure, Hartmann calls the stage which humanity is now approaching "manhood":[43] according to his description, however, that is the happy condition in which there is only "sterling mediocrity"[44] and art is "perhaps what an evening performance of a farce is to a Berlin financier",[45] in which

39. Eduard von Hartmann, *Philosophie des Unbewußten,* Berlin, 1869.

40. Friedrich Daniel Ernst Schleiermacher (1768-1834), German theologian and philosopher, one of the most influential thinkers of nineteenth century Protestantism.

41. Through efficient causes.

42. Through a final cause.

43. von Hartmann, op. cit., passim, especially pp. 619, 625.

44. von Hartmann, op. cit., p. 618.

45. von Hartmann, op. cit., p. 619.

"geniuses are no longer a requirement of the times because that would be to throw pearls before swine, or again because the times have advanced beyond the stage which deserved genuises to a more important one",[46] i.e., to that stage of social development in which each worker "leads a comfortable life with a workday which leaves sufficient leisure time to cultivate his intellect." Rogue of rogues, you express the yearning of contemporary mankind: but you also know which spectre will stand at the end of this manhood of mankind as a result of that intellectual education to sterling mediocrity—disgust. Evidently matters are quite wretched, but they will be much more wretched yet, "the antichrist is visibly extending his grasp further and further"[47] —but so it *must* be and so it *must* come, for with all this we are well on our way—to being disgusted with all existence. 'Therefore heartily forward in the world process as workers in the vineyard of the Lord, for the process alone can lead to redemption!'"[48]

The vineyard of the Lord! The process! To redemption! Who does not here see and hear historical education, which only knows the word 'become', as it intentionally adopts the guise of a parodic monster, as it says the most wanton things about itself through the grotesque mask it holds up! For just what does this last roguish appeal to the workers in the vineyard demand of them? In what work are they to strive forward heartily? Or, to put the question differently: what is left to do for the historically educated man, the modern fanatic of the process, swimming and drowned in the flow of becoming, in order to gather in the harvest of that disgust, the delectable grape of that vineyard? —He has nothing to do but to continue to live as he has lived, to continue to love what he has loved, to continue to hate what he has hated, and to continue to read the newspaper which he has read; for him there is only one sin—to live differently than he has lived. But how he has lived we are told, with the exaggerated distinctness of writing carved in stone, by that famous page with the sentences printed large which has transported the whole contemporary educational ferment into blind ecstasy and ecstatic rage because it believed it read in these sentences its own justification in an apocalyptic light. For of each individual the unwitting parodist demanded "the total surrender of personality to the world process for the sake of its goal, the redemption of the world";[49] or still more clearly: "the affirmation of the will to live is provisionally to be proclaimed as that which alone is correct; for only in the total surrender to life and its pains, not in cowardly personal resignation and withdrawal, is something to be achieved for the world process",[50]

46. von Hartmann, op. cit., p. 619.

47. von Hartmann, op. cit., p. 610.

48. von Hartmann, op. cit., p. 637-8.

49. von Hartmann, op. cit., p. 638.

50. von Hartmann, op. cit., p. 638.

"striving for individual abnegation of the will is just as foolish and useless, and even more foolish than suicide".[51] "The thoughtful reader will understand, even without further indication, what shape a practical philosophy erected on these principles will assume, and that such a philosophy cannot contain the estrangement from, but only the full reconciliation with life".[52]

The thoughtful reader will understand: and one could misunderstand Hartmann! And how unspeakably funny it is that one did misunderstand him! Shall we say that contemporary Germans are very perceptive? A doughty Englishman misses *delicacy of perception* in them, he even ventures to say *"in the German mind there does seem to be something splay, something blunt-edged, unhandy and infelicitous"*[53] —would the great German parodist contradict this? To be sure, according to his explanation we are approaching "that ideal condition in which the human race makes its history consciously": but evidently we are still a good distance from that perhaps still more ideal condition in which mankind will read Hartmann's book consciously. Once it comes to that no man will let the words "world process" slip through his lips unless these lips are smiling; for one will be reminded of the time when the parodic gospel of Hartmann was listened to, imbibed, disputed, venerated, propagated and canonized with the whole respectability of that *"German mind"*, even with the "distorted seriousness of an owl", as Goethe says. But the world must go forward, that ideal condition cannot be achieved by dreaming, we must fight and struggle to achieve it, and only through cheerfulness is there a way to redemption, the redemption from this misleading owlish seriousness. There will come a time when one will wisely refrain from all constructions of the world process or of the history of mankind, a time when one no longer considers the masses at all but once again the individuals who constitute a kind of bridge across the wild stream of becoming. These do not, as it were, continue a process but live in timeless simultaneity, thanks to history, which permits such co-operation, they live as the republic of geniuses[54] of which Schopenhauer speaks somewhere; one giant calls to the other across the bleak intervals of ages and, undisturbed by the wantonly noisy dwarfs who creep away beneath them, the lofty conversation of spirits continues. The task of history is to be the mediator between them and so again and again to provide the occasion for and lend strength to the production of greatness. No, the *goal of humanity* cannot lie at the end but only *in its highest specimens*.

51. von Hartmann, op. cit., p. 635-6.

52. von Hartmann, op. cit., p. 638.

53. The italicized passages are in English in the original. I have not found the source of the quotation.

54. Arthur Schopenhauer, *Neue Paralipomena*, Leipzig, Reclam, n.d, §517.

Our jester, of course, responds to this with that admirable dialectic which is just as genuine as its admirers are admirable: "As little as it would be compatible with the concept of development to ascribe an infinite past duration to the world process because in that case every conceivable development would already have been gone through which, after all, is not the case (oh rogue!), just as little can we concede an infinite future duration of the process; each would invalidate the concept of a development toward a goal (oh more of a rogue!) and would equate the world process with the Danaides' drawing water. The complete victory of the logical over the illogical (oh rogue of rogues!), however, must coincide with the temporal end of the world process, with judgment day."[55] No, you clear and mocking spirit, as long as the illogical still holds sway as it does these days, as long, for example, as one can still talk with general agreement of a "world process" as you do, judgment day is still far away: for it is still too cheerful on this earth, many an illusion still flourishes, for example the illusion of your contemporaries about you, we are not yet ripe to be flung back into your void: for we believe that things will become even more jolly once one has begun to understand you, you misunderstood unconscious one. But if, in spite of that, disgust should come with full force as you have prophesied it to your readers, if your depiction of your present and future should turn out to be correct—and no one has so despised both, despised with such disgust as you—then I will gladly be prepared to vote with the majority in the way proposed by you that next Saturday evening at precisely twelve o'clock your world is to end; and our decree is to conclude: beginning tomorrow there will be no more time and no more newspapers.[56] But perhaps it will have no effect and we will have decreed in vain: well, in that case we will at least not be short of time for a beautiful experiment. We take a balance and into one of the pans place Hartmann's unconscious and into the other one Hartmann's world process. There are people who believe that they will weigh the same: for each pan would contain an equally bad word and an equally good joke. —Once we understand Hartmann's joke no one will use his words about the "world process" anymore except as a joke. In fact it is high time to advance with a whole army of satirical malice against the aberrations of the historical sense, against the excessive delight with the process to the detriment of existence and life, against the thoughtless displacement of all perspectives; and we should always praise the author of the philosophy of the unconscious for being the first to succeed in clearly perceiving the ridiculous in the conception of the "world process" and, through the peculiar seriousness of his presentation, to make it possible to appreciate it even more clearly. What the "world" is there for, what "humanity" is there

55. von Hartmann, op. cit., p. 637.

56. The connection between time (Zeit) and newspaper (Zeitung) is lost in translation.

for is not to concern us for the time being, unless we want to be funny: for there just isn't anything funnier and more cheerful on the world's stage than the presumptuousness of those little worms called man; but do ask what you, the individual, are there for, and if no one else can tell you then just try sometime to justify the meaning of your existence *a posteriori*, as it were, by setting yourself a purpose, a goal, a "for this", a lofty and noble "for this". And perish in the attempt—I know of no better life's purpose than to perish, *animae magnae prodigus*,[57] in attempting the great and impossible. If, on the other hand, the doctrines of sovereign becoming, of the fluidity of all concepts, types and kinds, of the lack of any cardinal difference between man and the animal—doctrines which I take to be true but deadly—are flung at the people for one more lifetime in the current mania for education, then let no one be surprised if that people perishes of pettiness and misery, of ossification and selfishness, that is, if to begin with it disintegrates and ceases to be a people: it may then perhaps be replaced in the arena of the future by systems of individual egoism, fellowships intent on the rapacious exploitation of non-fellows and similar creations of utilitarian vulgarity. To prepare the way for these creations one need only continue to write history from the standpoint of the *masses* and to look in it for those laws which can be derived from the needs of these masses, that is, for the laws of motion of the lowest loam and clay strata of society. The masses seem to me worthy of notice in only three respects: first as blurred copies of great men, produced on bad paper with worn plates, further as resistance to the great, and finally as the tools of the great; beyond that, may the devil and statistics take them! What, statistics prove that there are laws of history? Laws? Yes, it proves how mean and disgustingly uniform the masses are: is one to call laws the effect of inertia, stupidity, aping, love and hunger? Well, we will admit it, but with that the following proposition is also sure: so far as there are laws in history, laws are worth nothing and history is worth nothing. But just this kind of history is now universally valued, the kind which takes the great mass drives to be the important and chief point of history and regards all great men only as the clearest expression, the bubbles, as it were, which become visible on the flood. Here the masses are, out of themselves, to give birth to greatness, that is, chaos is, out of itself, to give birth to order; and in the end, of course, the hymn to the birth-giving masses is intoned. Everything is then called "great" which has for a prolonged time moved such masses and which, as one says, has been "a historical power". But is that not quite intentionally to confuse quantity with quality? If the dull masses have found some thought or other, say a religious thought, quite adequate, tenaciously defend it and drag it through centuries: then and only just then the finder and founder of that thought is said to be great. But why! The noblest and highest has no effect on the masses; the historical

57. Approximately: having expended all one's mental energy.

success of Christianity, its historical power, tenacity and endurance, all this fortunately proves nothing as regards the greatness of its founder since basically it would testify against him: but between him and that historical success there is a very earthly and dark layer of passion, error, greed for power and honour, of the continuing effects of the *imperium romanum*[58] a layer from which Christianity drew that earthy taste and bit of soil which made possible its continuation in this world and, as it were, gave it its durability. Greatness is not to depend on success, and Demosthenes had greatness even though he had no success. The purest and most truthful adherents of Christianity have always questioned and impeded rather than promoted its worldly success, its so-called "historical power"; for they used to take a stand outside the "world" and did not concern themselves with the "process of the Christian idea", which is why they have mostly remained quite unknown and unnamed by history. Expressed in a Christian way: the devil is the regent of the world and the master of successes and progress; he is the real power in all historical power, and so it will essentially remain—even though this may ring quite painfully in the ears of an age which is used to the deification of success and historical power. For it is practiced in giving things new names and rechristening the devil himself. It is certainly the hour of a great danger: men seem to be near to discovering that the egoism of individuals, of groups or of the masses has at all times been the lever of historical movements; at the same time, however, one is in no way troubled by this discovery, but rather one decrees: let egoism be our god. With this new faith one prepares quite clearly and intentionally to erect coming history on egoism: only it is to be a prudent egoism, one which imposes a few restrictions on itself to achieve lasting security, one which studies history so as to get to know imprudent egoism. With these studies one has learned that the state has a quite special mission in the world system of egoism which is to be founded: it is to be the patron of all prudent egoisms in order, with its military and police force, to guard them against the terrible eruptions of imprudent egoism. For the same reason history too—namely as the history of animals and men—is carefully stirred into the dangerous, because imprudent, mass of the people and labouring strata, because one knows that a grain of historical education is capable of breaking rude and dull instincts and desires or to guide them onto the road of refined egoism. On the whole: man is now "giving thought to a practical, livable arrangement in his earthly home, one which prudently looks to the future",[59] as E. von Hartmann put it. The same author calls such a period the "manhood of man" and so ridicules what today is called "a man" as though only a sober selfseeker is understood by that; and he also prophesies a corresponding old age to follow such a

58. The Roman empire.

59. von Hartmann, op. cit., p. 618.

manhood evidently also only to vent his ridicule on those of our old men who are typical of the times: for he speaks of their ripe contemplative attitude with which they "overview the wild and stormy suffering of their past lives and comprehend the vanity of the former supposed goals of their striving".[60] No, to the manhood of that calculating and historically educated egoism corresponds an old age which clings to life with repulsive greed and without dignity, and then

> "The last scene of all
> That ends this strange eventful history,
> Is second childishness and mere oblivion,
> Sans teeth, sans eyes, sans taste, sans everything."[61]

Whether the dangers of our life and of our culture come from these vulgar, toothless and tasteless old men, or whether they come from those so-called "men" of Hartmann: against both of them we intend with our very teeth to hold fast the right of our *youth* and shall not tire to defend the future of our youth against those iconoclasts who would smash their image of the future. In this battle, however, we must make an especially distressing observation: *that the aberrations of the historical sense from which the present time suffers are intentionally furthered, encouraged and—used.*

And they are used against youth in order to train them to that manhood of egoism which is everywhere aspired to; they are used in order to break the natural aversion of youth with a transfiguring, that is scientific-magical illumination of that manly-unmanly egoism. One knows after all what history is capable of, owing to a certain preponderance one knows it only too well: of uprooting the strongest instincts of youth: fire, obstinacy, self-forgetting and love, of dampening the heat of its sense of justice, of suppressing or repressing its desire to ripen slowly with the counter-desire to be done quickly, to be useful quickly, to be fruitful quickly, of infecting honesty and boldness of feeling with doubt; it is even capable of defrauding youth of its fairest privilege, of its strength to plant within itself a great thought with brimful confidence and to let it grow out of itself into an even greater one. A certain excess of history is capable of all of this, we have seen it: through a continuous displacement of horizon-perspectives, through the elimination of an enveloping atmosphere it no longer permits man to feel and act *unhistorically*. From an infinite horizon he then retreats into himself, into the smallest egoistic region, and there must wither and dry up: probably he will attain to cleverness: never to wisdom. One can talk to him, he reckons with and is reconciled to the

---

60. von Hartmann, op. cit., p. 625. A phrase is dropped in the quotation.

61. W. Shakespeare, *As You Like It*, Act II, Scene VII.

facts, is not given to emotional outbursts, blinks and understands how to seek his own advantage or that of his party in the advantage and disadvantage of others; he unlearns superfluous modesty and so step by step becomes a Hartmannian "man" and "old man". But he *ought* to become that, just that is the meaning of what is now demanded so cynically, of the "total surrender of the personality to the world process"[62] —for the sake of its goal, of the redemption of the world, as E. von Hartmann, the rogue, assures us. Mind you, the will and goal of these Hartmannian "men" and "old men" can hardly be said to be exactly the redemption of the world: but surely the world would be more redeemed if it were redeemed from these men and old men. For then would come the realm of youth.—

10

Thinking of *youth* at this point I cry land ho! land ho! Enough and more than enough of this passionately searching and erring voyage on dark alien seas! Now a coastline is finally in sight: whatever it may be like we must land there, and the worst harbour of refuge is better than once again to stagger back into hopeless sceptical infinity. Let us just hold fast to land now; later we shall no doubt find the good harbours and make the approach of those who follow easier.

Dangerous and exciting was this voyage. How far are we now from the quiet contemplation with which we first saw our ship float out to sea. In tracking down the dangers of history we have found ourselves most severely exposed to them; we ourselves display the traces of those sufferings which, as a consequence of an excess of history, came over men of recent times, and precisely this treatise, as I will not conceal, shows its modern character, the character of weak personality, in the excess of criticism, in the immaturity of its humanity, in the frequent transition from irony to cynicism, from pride to scepticism. And yet I trust in the inspiring power which instead of a genius guides my vehicle, I trust in *youth* to have guided me correctly when now it *forces me to protest against the historical education of modern youth* and when in protest I demand that above all men must learn to live and use history only *in the service of the life they have learned to live.* One has to be young to understand this protest, and considering the early grey hair of our present youth one can hardly be young enough still to feel against what is really being protested here. An example will be helpful. Not much more than a century ago in Germany a natural instinct for what one calls poetry awoke in a few young people. Do we perhaps think that preceding generations as well as their contemporaries did not speak at all of that art which was alien and unnatural to them? We know the reverse: that with all their strength they

62. von Hartmann, op. cit., p. 638.

thought, wrote, quarrelled about "poetry" with words about words, words, words. The inception of that awakening to life of a word did not also spell the death of those word makers, in a certain sense they still live now; for if, as Gibbon[63] says, nothing but time, though much time, is required for a world to perish, so nothing but time, though much more time, is required for a false concept to perish in Germany, the "land of little-by-little". Nevertheless: there are now perhaps a hundred more people than a hundred years ago who know what poetry is; perhaps a hundred years later there will again be a hundred more people who in the meantime have also learned what culture is and that the Germans until now have no culture however much they may talk and strut about. They will find the general pleasure which the Germans take in their "culture" just as incredible and silly as we find it that Gottsched[64] was once recognized as classic or that Ramler[65] had the reputation of a German Pindar. They will perhaps judge that this culture was only a kind of knowledge about culture and quite a false and superficial knowledge at that. False and superficial, that is, because the contradiction between life and knowledge was endured because what is characteristic in the culture of truly cultured peoples was not seen at all: that culture can only grow and blossom out of life; while with the Germans it is only tacked on like a paper flower or poured over like icing and will for that reason always have to remain deceitful and unfruitful. The education of German youth, however, proceeds precisely from this false and unfruitful concept of culture: its aim, quite purely and loftily conceived, is not at all the liberally educated man but the scholar, the scientific man, namely, the scientific man who will be useful as soon as possible, who takes a position outside of life in order to know it quite clearly; its result, viewed in a mean empirical way, is the historico-aesthetic cultural Philistine, the precocious newly wise chatter box on matters of state, church and art, the sensorium of thousands of sensations, the insatiable stomach which yet does not know what honest hunger and

63. I have not found this reference in the *Autobiography* which seems to be the only book by Gibbon that Nietzsche ever read. A reading of *The Decline and Fall of the Roman Empire* makes it unlikely that the observation is actually from Gibbon. Of the four causes of the ruin of Rome which he identified (Ch. 71) he does not think "the injuries of time and nature" to be the most important or by themselves sufficient. He thinks that "the domestic quarrels of the Romans" were "the most potent and forcible cause of [Rome's] destruction" and calls the Coliseum, which figures as a symbol of Rome, "an edifice, had it been left to time and nature, which might perhaps have claimed an eternal duration."

64. Johann Christoph Gottsched (1700-1766), a German literary theorist and critic who introduced French eighteenth century classical standards of taste into German literature, especially drama. His most influential work *Versuch einer kritischen Dichtkunst für die Deutschen* was published in 1730. In that year he was appointed professor of poetry at the University of Leipzig and four years later became professor of logic and metaphysics.

65. Karl Wilhelm Ramler (1725-1798), a German poet who for forty-two years was professor of logic at the military school in Berlin and toward the end of his life (1790-1796) was director of the national theatre.

thirst are. That an education with that aim and this result is contrary to nature is felt only by the man who is not yet completely fashioned by it, it is only felt by the instinct of youth because it still has the instinct of nature which is first broken artificially and violently by that education. But whoever wants in turn to break this education must help youth to have its say, he must light the way for its unconscious resistance with the clarity of concepts and turn it into a conscious, loudly articulate consciousness. And how is he going to achieve such a strange goal?

Above all by destroying a superstition, the belief in the *necessity* of that educational procedure. It is, after all, a prevailing opinion that there is no other possibility at all than just our present tiresome actuality. Just examine the literature of higher education in the last decades with that in mind: the examiner will, with indignant astonishment, become aware how uniformly the whole intent of education is conceived in all the fluctuating proposals and vehemence of disagreement, how thoughtlessly the prevailing product, the "educated man" as he is understood at present, is accepted as the necessary and rational foundation of all further education. But that monotonous canon would read approximately thus: the young man has to begin with knowledge of culture, not even with knowledge of life and still less with life and experience itself. And this knowledge of culture is instilled or stirred into the youth as historical knowledge; that is, his head is filled with an enormous number of concepts which are drawn from the highly mediate knowledge of past ages and peoples, not from the immediate perception of life. His desire to experience something himself and to feel a coherent living system of his own experiences grow within—such a desire is anaesthetized and as it were intoxicated, namely with the rank illusion that it is possible in a few years to summarize within oneself the highest and most remarkable experiences of ancient times and precisely the highest times. It is the same absurd method which leads our young painters and sculptors into salons and art galleries rather than into the workshop of a master and above all into the sole workshop of the sole mistress, nature. As though one could cursorily amble around in history and so glean from past times their techniques and skills, the true harvest of their lives! As though life itself were not a craft which has to be learned from the beginning and continuously practiced without stint if it is not to breed a crawling brood of botchers and babblers!—

Plato considered it necessary that the first generation of his new society (in the perfect state) be educated with the help of a powerful *lie-in-need*; children are to learn to believe that all of them have already dwelled dreaming under the earth for a time where they were kneaded and shaped by the master artisan of nature. Impossible to rebel against this past! Impossible to oppose the work of gods! It is to count as an unbreakable law of nature: who is born as a philosopher has gold in his body, who as a guardian only silver, who as a worker only iron and bronze. Plato explains that just as it is not possible to mix these metals so it is not to be possible ever to topple and confuse the caste order; the belief in the *aeterna veritas*[66] of this order is the foundation of the new education and therewith of the new state. —And so the modern German too believes in the *aeterna veritas* of his education, of his kind of culture: and still this belief will fail, just as the Platonic state would have failed, if once the lie-in-need is confronted with a *truth-in-need*: that the German has no culture, because as a result of his education he cannot have it at all. He wants the flower without root and stem: that is, he wants it in vain. That is the simple truth, an unpleasant and rude, a real truth-in-need.

In this truth-in-need, however, *our first generation* must be raised; certainly it will suffer the most from this truth, for through it it must raise itself, and even itself against itself, into a new habit and nature out of an old and first nature and habit: so that it could talk to itself in old Spanish: "*Defienda me Dios de my*", God preserve me from myself, namely from the nature I have already acquired by my upbringing. It must taste this truth drop by drop, taste it as a bitter and violent medicine, and each individual of this generation must bring himself to a judgment about himself which as a general judgment about a whole age he would be able to endure more easily: we are without culture, still more, we are spoiled for living, for correct and simple seeing and hearing, for the happy grasping of the nearest and natural, and so far do not even have the foundation of a culture because we ourselves are not convinced of having a true life in us. Crumbled and fallen apart, on the whole half mechanically divided into an inside and an outside, sown with concepts as with dragon's teeth, engendering concept-dragons, in addition suffering from the sickness of words and without trust in any feeling of our own which has not yet been rubber-stamped with words: as such an unalive and yet uncannily active factory of concepts and words I may perhaps still have the right to say about myself *cogito, ergo sum*[67] but not *vivo, ergo cogito*.[68] Empty "being" but not full and green "life" is guaranteed me; my original feeling only guarantees that I am a thinking, not a living being, that I am not an *animal* but at most a *cogital*. First give me life and I will make you a culture from it! —so calls each individual of this first generation, and all these individuals will recognize each other by this call. Who will give them life?

No god and no man: only their own *youth*: unfetter it and you will have freed life along with it. For life only lay concealed, in prison, it is not yet

66. Eternal truth.

67. I think, therefore I am.

68. I live, therefore I think.

withered and dead—ask yourselves!

But it is sick, this unfettered life, and must be healed. Many ills ail it and it does not only suffer from the memory of its fetters—it suffers, so far as we are principally concerned here, from the *historical malady*. The excess of history has attacked the plastic powers of life, it no longer understands how to avail itself of the past as hearty nourishment. The malady is terrible, and yet! if youth did not have the clairvoyant gift of nature no one would know that it is a malady and that a paradise of health has been lost. This same youth also guesses with the curative instinct of that same nature how that paradise is to be regained; it knows the ointments and medicines for the historical malady, for the excess of the historical: and what are they called?

Do not be surprised, they bear the names of poisons: the antidotes to the historical are called—the *unhistorical and the superhistorical*. With these names we return to the beginnings of our essay and to their calm.

By the word 'the unhistorical' I denote the art and the strength of being able to *forget* and enclose oneself in a limited *horizon*: 'superhistorical' I call the powers which guide the eye away from becoming and toward that which gives existence an eternal and stable character, toward *art* and *religion*. *Science*—for it is science which would speak of poisons—sees in that force, in these powers, hostile powers and forces: for it only takes the observation of things to be the true and correct one, that is, to be scientific observation, which everywhere sees what has come to be, the historical, and nowhere being, the eternal; it lives in inner contradiction with the eternalizing powers of art and religion so far as it hates forgetting, the death of knowledge, so far as it seeks to remove all horizon-limitations and throws man into an endless-unlimited light-wave-sea of known becoming.

If only he could live therein! As in an earthquake cities collapse and become deserted and man erects his house on volcanic ground only hastily and trembling with fear, so life itself collapses into itself and becomes feeble and discouraged when the *concept-quake* which science provokes takes from man the foundation of his security and calm, the belief in the enduring and eternal. Now, is life to rule over knowledge, over science, or is knowledge to rule over life? Which of these two authorities is the higher and decisive one? No one will doubt: life is the higher, the ruling authority, for any knowledge which destroys life would also have destroyed itself. Knowledge presupposes life and so has the same interest in the preservation of life which every being has in its own continuing existence. Thus science requires a higher supervision and guarding: a *hygiene of life* is placed close beside science and one proposition of this hygiene would read: the unhistorical and the superhistorical are the natural antidotes to the stifling of life by history, to the historical malady. It is probable that we, the historically sick, will also have to suffer from the antidotes. But that we suffer from them is no proof that the treatment is incorrect.

And here I recognize the mission of that *youth*, that first generation of fighters and serpent slayers which precedes a happier and more beautiful culture and humanity without having more than an inkling full of promise of this future happiness and beauty to come. This youth will suffer from the malady and the antidote at the same time: and nevertheless they believe to be entitled to boast of stronger health and in general of a more natural nature than their forebears, the educated "men" and "old men" of the present. But it is their mission to shake the concepts which that present has of "health" and "education", and to generate ridicule and hatred against such hybrid concept-monsters; and the hallmark of their own robust health is to be just this that they, namely this youth, can themselves use no concept, no party slogans from the present store of current word and concept coinage to designate their own essence, but are only convinced at every appropriate moment by a power active in them, a fighting, eliminating and separating power, and by an ever heightened sense of life. One may deny that this youth already possesses culture—but for what youth would that be a reproach? One may speak of their lack of refinement and moderation—but they are not yet old and wise enough to know their place; but above all they need not feign and defend a ready-made culture and they enjoy all the consolations and privileges of youth, especially the privilege of courageous heedless honesty and the inspiring consolation of hope.

I know that these hopeful ones intimately understand all these generalities and that with their very own experience they will translate them for themselves into a doctrine meant personally; the others may meanwhile perceive nothing but covered bowls which may well be empty: until one day to their surprise they see with their own eyes that the bowls are full and that attacks, demands, drives to life, passions lay boxed up and pressed together in these generalities which could not remain covered long. Referring these doubters to time, which brings everything to light, I turn in conclusion to that company of hopeful ones to tell them in a parable the course and progress of their cure, their rescue from the historical malady, and so their own history to the point in time at which they will again be well enough to engage in studying history anew and to use history under the dominion of life in that threefold sense, namely monumental or antiquarian or critical. At that point in time they will be more ignorant than the "educated" of the present: for they will have unlearned much and moreover will have lost all inclination even to look at what those educated ones want to know above all; their distinguishing characteristics, seen from the perspective of those educated ones, are precisely their lack of education, their indifference and reserve toward much that is famous, even toward much that is good. But at that final point in their cure they have become *human* again and have ceased to be humanoid aggregates—that is something! Those are still hopes! Do not your hearts leap for joy at the thought, you hopeful ones?

And how do we arrive at that goal? you will ask. Already at the beginning of a journey to that goal the Delphic god calls his motto to you: "Know thyself". It is a hard motto: for that god "does not conceal and does not reveal, but only indicates"[69] as Heraclitus has said. What does he point out to you?

There have been centuries in which the Greeks found themselves in a danger similar to the one in which we find ourselves, namely of being swamped by what is alien and past, of perishing through "history". Never have they lived proudly untouchable: for a long time their "culture" was rather a chaos of foreign, Semitic, Babylonian, Lydian and Egyptian forms and concepts, and their religion a veritable battle of gods of the whole orient: similarly perhaps, as "German culture" and religion is now an internally battling chaos of all foreign countries, of all antiquity. And nevertheless Hellenic culture became no aggregate, thanks to that Apollinian motto. The Greeks learned gradually *to organize chaos* by reflecting on themselves in accordance with the Delphic teaching, that is, by reflecting on their genuine needs, and letting their sham needs die out. Thus they took possession of themselves again; they did not long remain the overloaded heirs and epigoni of the whole orient; after a difficult struggle with themselves and through the practical interpretation of that motto they even became the happiest enrichers and increasers of the inherited treasure and the firstcomers and models of all coming cultured peoples.

This is a parable for each one of us: he must organize the chaos within himself by reflecting on his genuine needs. His honesty, his sound and truthful character must at some time rebel against secondhand thought, secondhand learning and imitation; then he will begin to comprehend that culture can be something other still than *decoration of life*, that is, fundamentally always only dissimulation and disguise; for all adornment hides what it adorns. Thus the Greek concept of culture—in contrast to the Romance concept—will be unveiled to him, the concept of culture as a new and improved nature, without inside and outside, without dissimulation and convention, of culture as the accord of life, thought, appearing and willing. Thus he will learn from his own experience that it was through higher strength of *ethical* nature that the Greeks achieved a victory over all other cultures and that every increase of truthfulness must also be a preparatory advancement of *true* culture: even if this truthfulness may on occasion seriously harm the notion of culture which just then enjoys respect, even if it occasions the fall of an entire decorative culture.

69. Fragment B93.